The Mighty Queens *of* Freeville

For my family, and for the citizens
of my hometown
who have graced my life

Contents

CONTENTS

Acknowledgments

I NEVER UNDERSTOOD why writers were always thanking their agents, but now I do. Elyse Cheney helped me to find my voice. Without her help, encouragement, and representation, I would have wound up selling this book out of the trunk of my car at flea markets, along with a twelve-pack of tube socks.

Gretchen Young at Hyperion edited the book with grace, good humor, and Zen-like calm. I am so grateful. Hyperion reminds me of my hometown; it is a quirky community full of characters, and they all have my back. Ellen Archer leads by example, and I am honored to know her.

To anyone who has ever hired and paid me to do a job, I thank you—especially Jim Warren and Ann Marie Lipinski at the *Chicago Tribune*. I love being an advice columnist. If you hadn't hired me, I'd also be peddling my opinion out of the trunk of my car at flea markets.

ACKNOWLEDGMENTS

For the past fifteen years, I've had a home, professionally and personally, at National Public Radio. I've had the time of my life making radio.

Thank you to Jim Dicke, who supports the arts and artists through sustaining friendship.

For my sisters, Rachel and Anne. I look up to you both. My fear that you'll smack me with a hairbrush has kept me off the streets.

I thank my mother, Jane, and my daughter, Emily. You are peas in a pod—indulgent, funny, and kind. You both helped me to write this book and I am so grateful.

And to Bruno Schickel. Thank you, Bruno, for my happy ending.

The Mighty
Queens *of*
Freeville

Experience is, for me, the best teacher.

—CARL ROGERS, *psychologist*

Handsome is as handsome does.

—JANE DICKINSON, *my mother*

Introduction

ONE DECEMBER DAY in the mid–1980s, I looked out the front window of my mother's house and watched my soon-to-be husband walking up the road. He was carrying a newspaper and wearing a black chesterfield coat, leather gloves, and a fedora that had been custom blocked to fit his father's head by a milliner at Wanamaker and Company, sometime in the 1950s. He had left the house an hour earlier hoping to buy a *New York Times* at the Park-it-Market in the village. I knew that the periodicals rack at our small store held only copies of our local paper, the *Ithaca Journal*, along with *TV Guide*, *Guns & Ammo*, and a periodical that I had never dared to open, the ominously titled *Varmint Masters*.

My mother came up beside me. We watched as this man, who had never purposely set foot off a sidewalk, delicately picked his way through the ice and snow on our freshly plowed driveway.

"Hmmmmmm," she said. "He doesn't look like he's from around these parts."

This was true. He was born and raised on Manhattan's Upper East Side, but now he was in my neck of the woods, five hours north and a world away from Manhattan, in a place of pickup trucks and potbellied stoves and the occasional bathtub dumped on the lawn.

Later during our visit he asked my mother if there was anything that he could do for her. He was nice in that way. He knew how to behave. I'm not sure what he was really thinking at the time, but most likely his offer was one of those empty gestures that soon-to-be sons-in-law throw into the air like wedding confetti, hoping that they will briefly drift and swirl and blow quietly away.

My mother glanced around and then told him that if he wanted to, he could cut down a sapling that was growing in the front yard.

He climbed into his overcoat, pulled on his gloves, patted his hat into place, glanced in the mirror by the front door, and after a moment of reflection, took off his hat but decided to add a scarf. I ran out to the barn to retrieve the saw. I picked my way through the snow shovels, axes, rakes, hoes, and various other antique farm implements that were leftovers from our failed dairy farm, glanced at the old buckboard and carriage gathering dust in what used to be the stable, located the saw behind an old chest of drawers, and excitedly brought it to him.

Ten minutes later, he came back into the house, ruddy

and triumphant, as if he had spent the afternoon splitting kindling and shoeing horses. "I love being in the country!" he exclaimed. Out in the yard, the sapling lay toppled on the ground, right where it had fallen. Next to it stood its mighty trunk—four inches in diameter and three feet high. Half of the tree was still sticking up out of the ground, like a lone fence post in search of a fence.

He said that he didn't want to bend over.

Later, gloveless, hatless, and wearing my high school sweat-shirt for protection against the bitter winter wind, I snuck out and sawed the trunk down to ground level.

In my family, the women tend to do the heavy lifting while the men—well, the men are nice and fine and they love us for a time. Then at some point, it seems that they tire of their indeterminate role in our lives, so they wage a campaign of passive resistance, and then they leave.

I come from a family of women. Nature played its part (my mother is the youngest of four daughters and I am the youngest of three), but so did the tidal outflow of men in our lives. In time, my soon-to-be husband became an ex-husband, leaving me with—yes—a daughter to raise. And it is this daughter, Emily, now eighteen, who one day looked around at her family of women and declared us to be the Mighty Queens of Freeville.

Our realm, the village of Freeville (pop. 458), isn't much to look at. It's located on the northern fringes of Appalachia, in the rural and worn-out landscape of upstate New York. It's a town with one stop sign, anchored by a church, post office, elementary school, and gas station. There's a little diner called Toads, which seems to go in and out of business roughly on the same schedule as the floods that bedevil the creek that runs behind the village. (Toads and Fall Creek both seem to jump their banks on a regular basis.)

My family has called Freeville home for over two hundred years. We've tilled and cultivated the land, tended chickens and Holsteins, built houses and barns and backyard sheds. Most significantly, my family has made more family, and that's the main reason I continue to call this little place home. My mother, three aunts, two cousins, one of my sisters, three nieces, and a nephew all live in a tiny ten-house radius. My home offers one-stop shopping—family style. Though I've lived in New York City, London, Washington, DC, and now Chicago, for me, all roads lead back to my hometown.

My mother and two of my aunts raised their children alone. My two sisters, Rachel and Anne, were also single parents. When I got married, I deliberately tried to reverse the family's terrible marital track record, but failed. Afterward, I did what I do best—and what I've been doing off and on through my adulthood.

I went home.

The women of my family taught me what family is about. They helped me to pick up the pieces when my life fell apart, and we reassembled them together into something new. They celebrated my slow recovery, witnessed my daughter's growth and development, and championed my choices. The women in my life showed Emily and me in large and small ways that they would love us, no matter what. They abide.

Five years ago the *Chicago Tribune* announced that after a nationwide search they had chosen me to be "the next Ann Landers." My hometown paper, the *Ithaca Journal*, ran a front-page story about it. The *New York Times* and *Newsweek* wondered who I was and how I would be able to fill Landers's legendary shoes. Visits to the set of the *Today* show and CNN continued the query. Even Bill O'Reilly got into the act, bringing me onto his program in order to hector me about my family values.

In a town so intimate that people still talk about how gas station owner Bob Whyte once danced with Betty Grable at a USO show during World War II, making the front page of the *Ithaca Journal* is enough to catapult a person into the stratosphere of permanent local celebrity.

Now on my visits to Freeville, when I'm at the post office or at the diner, my hometown neighbors congratulate and kid me about my job. At the Freeville United Methodist Church, fellow congregants take up my column topics during Joys and Concerns, our public forum for prayer requests and blessings. When I'm doing my whites over at the Bright Day Laundromat, Joan, the owner, comments on my published opinions as she hands me my roll of quarters. During the summer, while I'm riding my bike down Main Street, cars pull over or honk and their drivers wave and yell, "Welcome home!"

But mostly when people see me, they ask the same question. They want to know how I know what I know. They want to know where my point of view comes from. I'm not a psychologist, therapist, or member of the clergy. I've never been the kind of person who has all the answers, though I do know where to get them. I've always been more likely to ask for counsel than to dole it out.

But at some point during the last five years, the balance tipped. My e-mail in-box now contains thousands of messages. My desk in Chicago is piled high with the last several days' servings of postal mail. The envelopes, crowded and tumbling, threaten to take over. I will open each and every one of them—eventually. I've turned in over two thousand columns now. On the job I've seen five years' worth of seasons come and go. I've fielded a basketful of queries from anxious brides and grooms, depressed fetishists, and long-distance lovers. I've communicated with kids, the elderly, baby boomers, and empty nesters.

The mail that pours in brings so many secrets, so many intimacies. In exchange for honoring me and trusting me by revealing their inner lives, my readers get my full attention, a lot of research and reporting, and a fair amount of quiet pondering. That's one reason people write to me—they need someone to do some thinking on their behalf. They need someone to be on their side or to talk them off the ledge. They want someone to hear them and to recognize that life can be a struggle. I do. But research and reporting don't answer the question of how I know what I know. That goes back to my family and this small town where I come from and to the fact that I—like most people actually—have had a life blessed with incident.

My family has been marked by our many losses. My brother, Charlie, has slipped from our lives, and I haven't seen him in ten years. My father is a distant memory. He walked away from our family and a barn full of livestock in 1972, and aside from occasional sightings, he is as gone as a person could be. My sisters and I all have ex-husbands who have exited from our family's life. We seem to be less than successful on many superficial levels. We don't have money. We aren't upwardly mobile. We aren't naturally thin or beautiful. We don't have advanced degrees, long-term career goals, or plans for retirement.

When talk about "family values" circles around and when politicians, religious leaders, and societal watchdogs trot out their examples of what a proper family is or should be, they're never talking about us. We are the "broken" ones. We are deep into the second generation of divorce. We are single women raising children. We are working mothers with kids in day care. And yet, when I think about actual family values—not the idealized version, but the kind that families like mine demonstrate—I realize that this highly imperfect and complicated family is quite functional. If it isn't perfect, then it is certainly good enough, and obviously very useful—certainly to me, since I make my living from drilling into the heart of other people's problems.

So when people ask me how I know what I know or

how I get to do what I do, I have the answer. I got here the hard way, by living a life and making my share of mistakes. I took the long way home, driving the back roads through marriage and divorce and raising a child on my own. But I got here with my family watching my back, with my hometown community influencing me and accepting my choices and enfolding me in their prickly embrace.

The Mighty Queens is the story of my family. Most especially, it is the story of my daughter, Emily, and me and of how we raised each other. In almost two decades of mothering her, I've made my share of mistakes. My daughter has watched me start and lose new careers and optimistically dab on mascara for yet another doomed blind date. She has caught me blowing fugitive cigarette smoke out the window and seen me wipe away my own tears with a paper towel while sitting, defeated, at the kitchen table. She has also witnessed the myriad and complicated joys of being in a family such as ours. And we taught each other how to have fun.

In my worst moments I fantasized about running from motherhood—but at the end of Emily's childhood, when it came time to say good-bye to her as she left home for college, I realized that mothering her had been the making of me. I am the product of my own upbringing, living in the shadow of my father's sudden departure during my childhood—but also witnessing my mother's surprise late-life success. I watched my own mother prevail, and my daughter has watched me prevail too. Fortunately for us,

Emily and I have grown up surrounded by the women who helped raise us.

My sisters and I get together now and then and go through our boxes of old photos—some are daguerreotypes and printed on glass or tin, some sepia-toned on crumbling paper—up through those taken with my mother's old Kodak Brownie, which are date-stamped with tiny black lettering along the prints' beveled edges.

There are photos of women wearing starchy Victorian blouses, bird-shaped hats, and lace-up boots; women with pinwheeling arms ice-skating on Fall Creek; women leaning against Chevy Impalas or pickup trucks, smoking cigarettes, with their arms flung around friends; women doing handstands on the lawn—or showing off their new babies, new shoes, or beloved house cats.

These are the women of my world—the Mighty Queens of Freeville—who have led small lives of great consequence in the tiny place that we call home.

ONE

Don't Throw Your Ring in the Creek

Surviving the Breakup

ONE DAY I looked out my front window and saw two big moving vans parked outside my house, pointed in opposite directions. Inside the house, two separate crews sifted through our family belongings according to color-coded Post-it notes.

That's when it dawned on me that I really *was* getting divorced.

Granted, the day my husband showed up at our marriage counseling session wheeling a suitcase, having just come in from a trip to Europe with his girlfriend, was a clue that our marriage was in trouble.

Other clues were when he told me that he no longer

loved me, followed by him saying that he didn't think that he had ever actually loved me. Followed further by comments he made about how after twelve years he had decided that we were too different and that we didn't want the same things in life and that, by the way, though he liked certain members of my family, he didn't like every member of my family. And how, since my father had left unceremoniously many years before, surely on some level I expected it to happen again?

These are the sort of conversational atrocities that stick with a person, and the thing about getting divorced is that you tend to spend a lot of time going over every single word that has ever been said pertaining to your relationship. Breaking up and getting together have that in common.

When I was first falling in love, I'd sit in the bathtub, slowly soaking, reviewing the events of the night before. What he said. What I said. His crinkly eyes. How I made him laugh. Did he say "I love you" or was it "I'm in love with you"? God, which was it? When I was falling in love, decoding the difference between those two statements was a full-time job.

When my marriage was ending, I'd sit in the tub quietly sobbing, hoping that I didn't wake the baby and wondering if secondhand smoke would seep under the door and get into her baby lungs. I'd just taken up smoking again, because if I was going to get divorced, then I might as well be a smoking, blowsy divorcée, a Joan Crawford divorcée.

We lived in London at the time, or as my mother used to

call it, "London, England." Living in a foreign country while you are getting divorced must be worse than living in your home country while you are getting divorced. Living in London, with its alienating plumbing and bowlegged furniture, was the worst of all.

I wanted two things when I first learned that my marriage was ending. First, I wanted it *not* to end. And second, I wanted for others to share a complete and interior knowledge of my heartbreak, followed by demonstrable grief. While there might be tiny streets tucked away somewhere in London where this sort of behavior is both possible and tolerated, they remain like Diagon Alley in the Harry Potter novels—attended by witches and warlocks and mysteriously hidden from view for the rest of us.

Like most Americans who live in jumping-off overseas posts, my husband traveled a lot for work, and he was gone much of the time. I lived in London because he lived in London, but unlike him I didn't have a job there. When I was asked what I did, which was infrequently, I said that I was a housewife. But I was less a housewife than a woman living on my own in a foreign country for no apparent reason.

We lived in a rented flat with rented furniture until I became pregnant and freaked out and then we bought (he bought) an apartment and furniture. And more furniture. And paintings. And rugs.

Shopping was my husband's favorite sport. He frequented galleries and stores the way the other husbands I knew hit golf courses. Our place quickly filled with his purchases—

items bought in souks and bazaars and galleries all over the hemisphere. Unfortunately his suitcase was more heavily used than our dining room table, which had once graced a farmhouse in France.

He would return from one of his many trips and I would catch him looking at the baby and me as if he were trying to place us. Had we met? Was it Vienna or the Ural mountains? Perhaps we had crossed the English Channel aboard the same hovercraft? He never learned the rhythm of our home. He didn't remember that our baby, Emily, took her long nap in the morning or that she liked to swing with the other babies on those little swings at the park—the ones that look like little buckets.

The traveling and frequent absences became the most obvious reason for the death of our marriage, but I thought the real problem was that my husband didn't know how to be in a family. He grew up in a tiny family that was silent and alien. His parents had gone through one of those ugly New York City divorces when he was little. He told me that when he was still in grade school, he and his older brother had been compelled to testify in court, each speaking for an opposing parent.

Having grown up on a failed dairy farm in rural poverty of the ugly, muddy sort, I envied his material polish and his Walter Pidgeonesque charm, some of which came naturally, supplemented by years in boarding school, and yet I felt sorry for him on the family score. He had one brother and only one cousin. He and his brother and their parents

and stepparents floated in separate orbits, sometimes inter-
secting briefly around the holidays. When he was a boy, he
would travel by cab on Christmas morning from his mother's house in the East 60s to his father's apartment twenty
blocks away. Ever since learning this, I imagine New York
City on Christmas morning as being full of taxis occupied
by depressed shuttling children adhering to court-ordered
holiday visitation.

My family is large and loud and abnormally weighted
down by women. My mother and her three sisters all live in
my tiny hometown, along with my two sisters, their children, and several cousins. He always said that he loved that
about me—that I was part of a package overflowing with
people who could populate his piddling world.

Though divorce runs through my clan like an aggressive
chromosome, I had never been exposed to family ugliness
of any sort, partly because my parents' divorce happened
after my father simply and suddenly walked away from our
home. I never saw my parents argue before, during, or after
their split. One advantage to actual abandonment is that it
cuts down on marital discord. In order to fight with my
father, my mother would have had to locate him first.

After my father left, my mother spent about a year telling
her four adolescent children that everything was going to
be OK, as we lost and lost and then lost some more. Even
though he drove away in his pickup truck with only his
clothes wadded up in a paper bag from the IGA, my father
managed to take everything with him. It turned out that

his life—and our little dairy farm—was leveraged to the hilt. Though my mother was able to hold on to our house, we lost everything else, first in a rush and then in a Chinese water torture trickle of receivership. Even our small herd of cows was repossessed.

It's an old-fashioned notion to even try to maintain one's dignity in the face of outrage, but I watched my mother do her best. Exercising her only marketable skill, she got a job as a typist in an office. She was forty-two and had been a full-time farm wife and mother for twenty-two years. At night she would come home from work and lie down on her bed still wearing her coat, holding her purse across her stomach.

"I just need twenty minutes," she would say. Then she would hoist herself up, walk into the kitchen, and start cooking supper. After years of preparing large meals featuring homegrown produce and homemade breads and preserves—always followed by a baked dessert—my mother stepped down to hot dogs served on buns pulled from plastic sleeves, accompanied by potato chips.

My father had limited interest in his children, so there was no question of custody. My mother never pursued him for any sort of financial support—and he didn't offer it.

She simply prevailed. Prevailing is underrated. People have the idea that unless they win, they lose. But sometimes surviving is enough. My mother knew this, and I learned it by watching her.

Before he left, my husband was grouchy for about a week.

He had always been extraordinarily nice to me, so I jumped through hoops of decreasing circumference trying to get him to be nice again. But then he picked a fight with me about Benazir Bhutto—who in the late 1980s was Pakistan's newly elected prime minister—and I knew that we had turned a corner and wandered into the volatile Middle East of our marriage. Granted, in general I think that looking to Pakistan for common ground in a relationship is probably a sign it is ending. The State Department should be called. Diplomats should get involved. I realized that my husband was amassing troops along his border. It would only be a matter of time before a trigger-happy infantryman fired the first shot that would start the war.

Despite my efforts, the week before he left me, my husband drifted into a slumber state. He went to bed very early and then slept until noon each day. Emily was going through a phase of waking up at 5 A.M., and I would get up with her, get breakfast, drink two pots of coffee, play with her in her room, put her down for her nap, get her up again, take her out for a walk, and then wander around, looking at our tasteful apartment until he finally emerged from our bedroom.

On the day he said he was leaving, it was 2 P.M. and he had just come out of the shower. I got mad at him. I told him that I had lived an entire lifetime while he slept and bathed and carefully groomed himself. I said that I was worried about him because he seemed depressed. (Though honestly, he looked great. He had recently lost weight and was working out at a fancy gym on Fulham Road.)

He sighed.

Then he said that he was leaving. At first I thought he meant he was leaving the house. Then I realized he was leaving the marriage.

After a full day and night of crying interrupted by sobbing, I called my friend Betsy—the one friend I had in London—and told her that my husband was leaving. She didn't believe me. It is fairly awful to have to assure someone that one of the worst things you can think of happening has actually happened. People who wish you well can't believe your bad news any easier than you can. Betsy instantly loathed my husband, who she had always liked and admired, and called him bad words because I couldn't.

I learned early on in my divorcing process that I could not say bad words pertaining to my husband. Yesterday I had loved him deeply. Today when I woke up I still loved him deeply until I remembered that he was leaving me. Then I didn't know what to think or how to feel. I just wanted to stay married. Marriage was an assumption I had made about my life and I couldn't simply undo it. Even though I had had a short career as a journalist, marriage and motherhood were the jobs I thought I would do best. Marriage and motherhood were my life's work.

I wanted my husband to hurry up and get over leaving me and come back so that I could forgive him for leaving. Then we could stay married and turn into one of those older and wiser couples who have been through hard times together but whose relationship had grown stronger because of it—the kind of couple they profile in *Redbook* magazine.

Even though I had always pictured myself as someone who would kick ass first and ask questions later, one of the many lessons my divorce taught me was that I was more willing to forgive than I had ever thought possible—certainly if forgiveness was the path to getting what I wanted. I thought that if I forgave him for leaving me, then he wouldn't leave me. Then we'd get back together, maybe move back to the States and buy a little place on Cape Cod because we'd survived this close call and learned our lesson.

Instead, he moved to a hotel near his office, but he wouldn't tell me which one. He said he would be in touch and that, of course, I could always reach him at work. He seemed afraid of me. I'm not sure what he thought I would do, because in order to follow him anywhere, I would have had to bring a baby, a stroller, diaper bag, a bottle, some snacks, and of course a couple of those little cardboard books that she liked to page through whenever we went out.

I cried on an eighteen-hour schedule, taking breaks only to sleep and smile at the kindly Indian shopkeepers in our neighborhood who were always nice to Emily and me. When I wasn't crying, I took very long baths, soaking in tepid bubbles and ruminating on my heartache.

When his mother called the house, asking for him, I realized that he hadn't told anyone in his family and that most likely he wanted me to do it. I lied and took a message for him.

Betsy came over and held Emily. "Is there someone else?" she asked.

"Not possible," I said.

But she had opened the door, and then I started thinking about it.

I got a sitter and went to his office. I said hello to the receptionist and walked down the hallway. They were re-modeling the interior of the building and the place was a construction zone. I stood outside his open office door. He was on the phone. He looked at me in that absent way people have when they're otherwise engaged and, still talking, walked around the desk and quietly but slowly shut the door in my face.

I sat on a sawhorse and waited. Somebody asked me if I wanted a cup of coffee.

I did not.

After about twenty minutes, the office door opened and I was gestured in.

I pulled a bluff-calling maneuver that I had once seen on *Columbo*.

"I know about her," I lied. "You've been lying and lying to me, and now it's time to tell the truth. You might as well."

He did.

"You're an idiot," I said. Then I went home.

I entertained active fantasies about her. She was much younger than the two of us and had turned our family into a cliché. I didn't want to meet her as much as I wanted to hire somebody to run her over with a car while I watched from a café across the street.

I wanted to shame her, to call her parents and report to them what their daughter had done with her life in her first year out of college. I wanted to place this call while the baby cried in the background. I rehearsed the scene obsessively in my mind, but since Emily was extremely quiet, I knew that I would probably have to pinch her to get her to cooperate and cry on cue.

I took Emily and flew to my mother's house in the States. I cried some more on the plane. I knew that I would have to tell my mother what had happened. My mother loved my marriage almost as much as I did. I think that she saw in it the possibility that a good marriage would affect the family's relationship karma.

"Oh dear," she said. "I couldn't be more surprised. Dear, dear." She patted me like a cat as we sat on the porch together.

At night, I lay in bed in the back bedroom of my mother's house next to my snoring daughter, looking out at the landscape that had once been our farm and listening to the peepers pulse and sing on the creek. I remembered that after my father left, my mother would take her coffee and sit on our front steps, smoking cigarettes, listening to the peepers and playing the Three Dog Night song "Out in the Country" over and over on our stereo.

Fifteen years after her divorce, though, my mother had made something of her life. After her children left home, she went to college and then graduate school. She became a professor and paid off the debts my father had left behind.

My father was on his fifth marriage and had lived, briefly, in his van.

For the first time in my adult life, I started to think about the kind of person that I really wanted to be. If I let it, I realized that my divorce could turn me into a vengeful goddess of unremitting heartache. But I wanted to be decent. I wanted to be kind. I wanted to feel good about my own behavior, because everything else felt so bad. I wanted to do something right.

I left my mother and went back to London.

My cousin Roger called me. He said he had just heard about what had happened and he wanted to tell me that he was willing to fly to London in order to punch my husband in the nose. He is one of the few men in my family, and I appreciated this brotherly show of solidarity. It remains one of the nicest things that anyone has ever offered to do for me. I thanked him and told him that if it ever came to that, I would punch my husband myself and tell him: "Roger sent me."

The shock of my news started to wear off and I settled into a state of depression punctuated by periods of high anxiety as I tried to figure out what would become of us. My husband made halfhearted attempts to come back home. He would feel bad and show up at our place with flowers from the supermarket. He'd sit in our living room and watch me cry, then go back to his hotel.

Thinking I might have a chance with him again, I said that perhaps we needed to spend time together. We got Betsy to watch Emily for a few days and went on that trip to Italy we'd been putting off.

It was too late. We broke up in Rome and then again on Capri. Our breakup was becoming a globally depressing drama, with spectacular backdrops. As always, we didn't fight. We just took turns giving up. He was grouchy and, I assumed, mooning over his girlfriend, whose address and phone number I located on a page in his address book. I tore out the page, crumpled it up, and tossed it out the window.

EVEN THOUGH I suspected that our marriage was quite over, I didn't trust myself to know that. I wanted a witness. I found a marriage counselor. My husband said he would meet me at the appointment, but I could tell that it was a courtesy. When I saw him in the foyer of the therapist's office, it was clear that he hadn't exactly been pacing with nerves, losing sleep, and chain-smoking the way I had been. He had just come from a trip and seemed—how to put it—happy.

Like every therapist in the movies, our therapist wore a flowing muumuu dress and chunky jewelry. My husband opened by telling the woman how stale our marriage was. How trapped he felt. He used the word *nag*. That was when

I realized that marriage counseling might not go exactly the way I wanted. I wanted to have a tender experience whereby everyone would be made to understand my point of view and where my rage and hurt would be acknowledged. I wanted my status as heartbreak victim to be confirmed. And I wanted an apology.

In that room I saw that if I was going to air my heartache for him, then he would air my deficits and the depths of his dissatisfaction for me. I knew that I would not get my husband back, but that we would be left with the intimate knowledge of the details surrounding the disintegration of our marriage. We had a child to raise, and there was a limit to how bad I was willing to feel about myself and her father while doing it.

I remembered a story my mother had told me. My father left her with nothing and then when she learned from the bank that he had mortgaged our farm, she found out that it was actually possible to leave someone with less than nothing. Later that day she stood on the bank of Fall Creek, which flows in gentle and wide curves through the land where we once grew crops and cows. She took off her engagement ring—a pretty little thing that my father had purchased in 1950—and cocked her hand back to throw it into the creek.

She used to laugh when she told this story. She would point out the absurdity of making such an empty gesture when at the end of it, she'd still have less than nothing. The only thing different would be that a nice little ring would be lying on the creek bottom.

Save yourself, I thought.

I TURNED TO my husband.

"I release you," I said.

"Huh?" he said. We generally didn't talk like that.

"I release you. I'm done."

I could tell that he wanted to run off and find a phone booth in order to call his girlfriend. Instead, he took out a little notebook, and we started to divide our stuff into column "you" and column "me." I discovered that I didn't care too much about any of it, so he got the French farmhouse dining room table.

I said I'd take the chairs.

I found a mediator to meet with the two of us, and we kept the lawyers out of it. We learned how to talk like dispassionate accountants, which was fine because we had business to do and things to negotiate. He didn't want our child to be dragged around as he had been at Christmastime, so he didn't insist on seeing her over the holidays. I wanted our daughter to have a father in her life because my father hadn't been in mine, so I told him that I would help him be a father to her—not on my terms, but on his.

We found that we'd both learned about divorce from our parents, and if we weren't able to subvert history and rearrange our futures enough to have a happy marriage, then at least we could have a good divorce.

I decided to forgive him, though it was way too soon to do so and I didn't know if I was ready. But I decided to forgive him anyway. Forgiveness didn't work the way I thought it would. First of all, it wasn't a natural impulse, and even though in my life I have been a practicing Methodist, Presbyterian, and Episcopalian, forgiveness wasn't quite the spiritual experience that I had been taught it would be. Forgiveness, it turned out, was a choice that I had to make, not to get him to come back, but in order to let him go. Whether it meant anything to my husband or if he even noticed it, I don't know. That wasn't the point.

The day the moving vans came, our little family stood together, quietly watching our belongings toted out of the house by teamsters. I imagine that moving men witness an awful lot in their job as people play out the joy and anxiety they feel as they contemplate leaving one place and moving to another. Our two moving crews were quiet. They slipped in and out quickly. I told myself that if I had cared too much about material things before, I never would again. I didn't care if the container holding our stuff fell off the ship carrying it across the Atlantic.

The vans pointing in opposite directions on the street said it all. I was taking Emily, now a toddler, back to the States. We would live in my sister's spare bedroom in my hometown until I could figure out what to do next. He was moving to Russia. He said that he would see our daughter when he could, and though I wondered when that would possibly be—given the distance, his schedule, and his fear of running into my cousin Roger's fist—I tried to believe him.

On our flight to the States, our jumbo jet hit a wave of extreme turbulence as we passed through the jet stream. The flight attendants locked down the cabin and strapped themselves into their seats. I was terrified. I've always been a very nervous flier, and at the slightest sign of trouble I lurch into a state of high anxiety, complete with flop sweat and the fear of passing out, or worse—the peeing of one's pants. The plane was bucking and I thought I could feel it twisting.

I tightened my seat belt and unconsciously felt along my daughter's tummy to make sure that hers was snug. I looked out at the other passengers. Though to me they looked exactly like the cast of a television disaster movie—executives, a children's choir coming back from a competition in Scotland, and a nun wearing a habit—they didn't seem to realize that they had been cast in my disaster. They seemed calm. Of course, I thought, they don't know what I am going through. They don't know that I couldn't make my husband love me anymore and that I am headed back to my cruddy little hometown to try and build a new life from my sister's spare bedroom.

Nobody—not a single one of these people—knows how to make love stay.

My daughter tugged my sleeve.

My God. I am a *single mother*.

"Weeeeeee Mommy!" She looked up at me with eyebrows raised and a huge, expectant smile. "Roller coaster!"

Jesus. She looked exactly like her father. I laughed.

"Yes. That's right. Roller coaster."

TWO

Tea Alone

On Mothering without a Net

I T WAS MARCH in Freeville.

My little hometown had been worked over by winter's harsh blasts, and now the rains—cold, hard, and unrelenting—had arrived to finish the job. The trees lining Main Street were iron-colored skeletons, and without foliage or winter's massive snowbanks to camouflage them, the clapboard houses looked tattered and sagging.

My sister Rachel pushed her daughter Railey's toys out of the way and gave us Railey's bedroom in the back of the minuscule two-bedroom bungalow just off Main Street that she had bought the year before.

Emily and I moved in. I had nowhere else to go and no

plans beyond a vague idea that I would somehow wait for my fortunes to change.

More important than the loss of my current fortunes, though, was the way my future had changed shape. Geometry no longer described our family. We used to be a triangle: Mommy, Daddy, Baby. Now Emily and I were two points, connected by a thread. We used to be a group—my husband, daughter, and me. Now I was part of a couple. Our lives once had a forward trajectory. Now I was blown back into my own past.

Our first few days in Freeville involved lots of coffee drinking and toilet paper. We are not Kleenex people, so when it looked like my case of chronic crying might in fact be terminal, Rachel gave me my own roll of Charmin, which I worked down to its cardboard tube.

Rachel and I had to speak in code because Railey was both precocious and a blabbermouth. We didn't want my niece's pre-K class to be treated to the details of my marriage's disintegration, so many of our conversations went like this:

"I really want to call him."

"Don't call him."

"OK. After today I won't call him."

"Don't call him today, either."

"Well, I already called him today but he didn't answer."

"Good God. Well, don't call him tomorrow, then. Jesus, can't I leave you alone for a minute?"

"Please don't."

My relatives littered Freeville like downed tree limbs after a storm. The village's population of 458 had remained stagnant since the 1930s—my family's own population growth had filled in gaps left by death and attrition as residents gave up on the region's October-to-April winters and moved to Florida. At that time my other sister, four cousins, three aunts, and mother lived within a short distance of Rachel's house. My cousin Jan, sisters Anne and Rachel, and I had had our kids one after another, so our combined six children were ages two to six.

My family started to circle. It was like the scene in *The Wizard of Oz* where Glinda the good witch asks the shy Munchkins to come out to meet Dorothy. "Come out, come out, wherever you are . . . ," she trills, and so my family emerged from their homes up and down Main Street, tentatively at first—because no one knew what to say—and then more boldly as they discovered that it didn't really matter; I wasn't quite ready to listen. I just wanted a soft place to fall.

Emily became acquainted with her young cousins in my sister's tiny living room that soggy March, and they engaged her in the hand-to-hand combat that was their particular style of play. Since I had only one friend in London with a child Emily's age, she had never really played with other children before. This was play as a full-contact sport, and my mother and I (both softies) would wince as Emily was repeatedly trampled.

"Well, you have to think that maybe this will toughen her up," Mom offered helpfully, after four-year-old Nathan rammed her with his Big Wheel. (Nathan menaced the village on his Big Wheel like a teenager in a Camaro.)

"You mean the idea 'that which doesn't kill me makes me stronger'?" I offered as I scooped up my toddler to comfort her. I could see the utility of that way of thinking and of course wondered if I should apply that theory to myself. The problem is, I can't for the life of me figure out what's so great about being tough in the first place.

I had no ideas and no prospects, so I behaved like the housewife I had become during my marriage. I took care of Emily, cleaned my sister's house while she was at work, walked her dog, and hung out with Railey when she came home after school. Emily and I walked to the post office on Main Street each day and stopped at the village store for a treat. In the evenings we would visit with Mom.

My mother's lovely little house on Mill Street is filled with comfortable furniture and family things passed down through generations of our clan. Among her possessions were toys my grandfather had played with during his Freeville childhood almost a hundred years ago, including a tin stagecoach, which Emily placed dolls on and pushed around the kitchen floor. A portrait of a glowering ancestor menaced visitors from the living room.

Mom and I sat at her kitchen table, drinking coffee and watching Emily engage in play that, in this age of plastic, seemed pulled from another time. Mom had purchased a set of wooden alphabet blocks for Emily to play with, and I noticed that my mother had set them up on the windowsill of the kitchen to spell:

T-E-A

A-L-O-N-E

"So, what do you think you're going to do?" my mother asked one evening.

"Do? You mean tomorrow? I think I'm going to take Emily over to the Marquis farm to see them make maple syrup."

"No; what are you going to do next?"

"Next? I don't know."

I didn't have a "next" yet.

One morning a week, my family gathered at Toads diner at the edge of the village for breakfast. My extended family members are in the habit of visiting with one another constantly—even though they see one another almost daily, they still feel the need to punctuate the week with planned get-togethers.

At Toads, we'd pull up high chairs and booster seats and three generations of us would talk over one another until the last pancake was eaten and the coffee had run cold. In the presence of my mother, three aunts, cousins, sisters, and our children, I started to remember who I was before I'd had the stuffing knocked out of me.

I come from a family of women who have a lot to say. In

fact, my mother and her three sisters, Lena, Millie, and Jean, have been engaged in a conversation about nothing in particular that started in 1929. To successfully track a typical encounter with the four of them would require a team of linguists with clipboards and sensors, feeding streams of data into a supercomputer.

Conversational categories include:

Ancestor Trivia
Politics and You
Jellies and Preserves
Movies, Books, and Popular Culture
Humidity
Law & Order **(the television show)**
Pets: Dead or Alive
Snow Removal
Cold and Ice
Offspring
Curtains

The only topic I can think of that my mother and aunts will never broach comfortably is talking about other people. A hint of gossip and the needle scratches across the record. They go silent. They also don't like to talk about themselves, but they will happily talk about you to you and ask you questions about yourself. This is probably why I have always felt fascinating when I'm around them; I develop a case of self-enchantment that I can't help but associate with being in their presence.

Of my mother and her three sisters, only my aunt Lena had managed to stay married, though she was hardly smug on this topic. Aunt Lena's very long marriage to my uncle Harvey was seen as a glitch in the clan's otherwise perfect record of going it alone. My mother and aunts Millie and Jean had all been single mothers. Being with them reminded me that it could be done.

Though I doubted I'd ever be comfortable anywhere, I considered settling down permanently in my hometown. At the very least, I knew what life there would be like. Generations of my family had grown up, grown old, and died alongside generations of the other families in Freeville.

In small towns, everybody knows where the bodies are buried—literally. Our town cemetery contains headstones bearing the names of local families, and I know the intimate details and familial backstories of many of them. Of course the downside to knowing your neighbors' stories is that they know yours too.

When my father abruptly departed from our family in order to run off with a truck stop waitress, his behavior was scandalous enough that I was aware of the news circulating around us in murmurs. The talk was like snowfall—everywhere and impossible to dodge. Our small dairy farm failed in agonizing stages as a result of my father's leaving, and one day all of our farm equipment—including the leftover hay stacked inside the barn—was sold in an auction attended by a couple hundred people, many of them neighbors and families that my siblings and I went to school with.

I was twelve. I hated the idea that so many people were witnessing the worst day of my childhood.

I came of age in an era when people openly referred to households of divorce as "broken homes." During my small-town adolescence, my parents' divorce and my family's broken-ness were the awkwardness that I could never shake, so I papered it over with accomplishments and certificates and prizes. I sang. I danced. I ran endless laps around various sports fields, chasing balls of every size and shape. I campaigned for office and served on decorating committees. I was very busy keeping busy.

Now, thirteen years after my triumphant turn around the football field as Dryden High School's class of 1977's Homecoming Princess, I was home again, and my life had slowed down so much that I was actually moving backward.

I didn't even sleep in a grown-up's bed.

One day I borrowed my mother's car and drove to the bank in Dryden, three miles away. My separation agreement had come from London in the mail and I needed to have it notarized. (If the first stage in becoming a single mother is the dramatic emotional part—the crying, making up, breaking up, and more crying—then the second stage is all about shame and paperwork.)

A chilly rain was melting the dirty but diminishing

snowbanks lining every road and parking lot. I unhitched Emily from her borrowed car seat and tucked her—along with the documents giving me full and legal custody of her—under my coat as I dashed into the bank.

My hometown bank was last renovated in 1967 and is a gem of period fieldstone decor and burnt orange wall-to-wall carpeting. Four of the six tellers were named "Tammy." The Tammies stood expectant at their banking stations. They sported the poodle-fronted she-mullet hairdos of small-town beauty queens and country-and-western singers that were popular at the time. I went to high school with most of them. I went to high school with the older siblings of the rest of them.

I was directed toward the back of the building where the notary public sits. Carla was in Rachel's class in school. Her parents had grown up with my parents. I looked up to her the way I looked up to my sister, though in Carla's case it was purely because she was older and had been a standout on our high school swim team.

Carla examined my documents, then looked at me and then at Emily. "So you're moving back home?" she asked as she pulled her stamp out of its velvet-lined case.

She didn't mean anything by it. She was just making conversation.

On the way home, after I stopped crying, I pulled the car over to the side of the road. Emily had fallen asleep in her car seat. I adjusted the rearview mirror in order to look at her. Her head was cocked at an impossible floppy drunken angle, and I wondered why toddlers so often slept like that, yet never seemed to have neck aches. I turned off the windshield wipers and let the rain sluice down the windshield. I closed my eyes.

If I stayed in my hometown, I would run into people who knew too much about me for the rest of my life. I would be the ex-cheerleader and former "most likely to succeed" who didn't quite make it. I would be a second-generation member of a *broken home*.

I felt I was living a life that seemed pulled from a movie on the Lifetime channel. Even though I had always been told that I bore a passing resemblance to the actress Valerie Bertinelli, I had a horror of providing the plot for a Valerie Bertinelli movie ("Tonight on Lifetime: *Not Without My Daughter!*"). Nor did I want to live in fear of running into one of the Tammies.

I wanted to write the next chapter of my story, and so for the first time in a very long time, I made what felt like an actual decision. I chose to settle in the last place where I had been on my own—before marriage, parenthood, and divorce.

I went to college in Washington, DC, and then stayed on to work there for three years after graduation. I still had some friends there and thought I'd be able to find a job.

That night I asked Rachel what she thought. "Yes," she said. "That sounds just right."

It took a month to figure out where to live. It took another month to say good-bye.

By May, spring had finally come to Freeville, and the trees were smeared with peridot-colored leaves. Daffodils rose in clumps along the banks of Fall Creek. Our neighbor Dave had removed his shirt—Dave takes off his shirt on the first warm day and doesn't put it back on until October. In Freeville, seeing Dave's torso as he works in his yard is the first sign of spring. "Well, I see Dave's shirtless—I guess it's time to plant the flower boxes and get the bikes out of the barn," my mother said.

Rachel and I packed a rental car with the luggage Emily and I had brought from London. On our way out of town, we stopped at Mom's house and she gave me and Emily a hug. "I love it when the trees are in leaf," I said to her.

"Yes, and now you are leafing too," my mother replied. Then she said, "See you in ten minutes at Toads?"

Sure.

The whole family was there, crowded around our usual table. I told them we'd be back constantly. It was only a seven-hour drive.

Rachel moved us into our little apartment in Washington on a hot day at the beginning of a summer that turned out to be full of stifling days. She took a look around our rental, pointed out all of its great qualities, and, just before she left, declared the rest of our life ready to begin.

I wasn't so sure.

Emily was two years old, I was thirty-two and I felt that my life was leftover, tattered, and grimy, just like the furniture that crowded us in our too-small place. Still I dug into boxes that had followed me to New York and then London but that hadn't been opened since I packed my possessions after college. I pulled out my old rotary telephone. It had a jangly, exhausted ring, but it still worked. I found an old answering machine. It had been packed away just after our honeymoon—before my new husband and I moved to England. I played the five-year-old messages on the tape. Sitting on the floor, surrounded by boxes, I listened to a string of messages congratulating us on our marriage and wishing us a safe and happy honeymoon trip.

I set up Emily's bedroom in the little side room that was supposed to be the apartment's den. Four floors up, it had a wall of windows that faced a heavily wooded gully that ran beside our building. The view, all green and leafy, made you feel as though you were sitting in a tree house. We settled into a routine. Friends from college who had stayed in DC rallied around us in a loose group. One of them who had a son Emily's age told me about a swimming pool where you could join for a small fee.

All through that hot and steamy summer, the pool was our daily destination. I would pack lunches and books and head out in the morning, before it got too hot. Emily splashed with the other toddlers in the small round kiddy pool, and I would sit thigh to thigh with the other mothers, dangling our legs in the warm water.

I was trying to find a way to reenter the world. Because thinking about my own experience exhausted me, I spent much of my time at the pool listening to suburban moms complain about their husbands. The thrust of their issues seemed to be that they could not get their husbands to do what they wanted them to do. And when their husbands did something that they wanted them to do, they did it badly.

Single parenthood is hard, but it's simple too.

You just do everything yourself.

Doing everything yourself has a way of relaxing a person's standards. The kinds of things that drove me crazy during my marriage—my husband's passive incompetence or indifference when it came to certain childrearing chores— didn't seem quite so devastating when I was at fault. Undercooking the macaroni, skipping a nap, not changing a diaper on time, or falling asleep during a bedtime story didn't seem like such a crime when I committed it.

As a person headed out of marriage, I started viewing these unions differently. When it comes to raising children, I wonder how well the average marriage really works. Along with a second pair of hands that couples get when they're married, they also get two styles, speeds, and sets of values. I missed many things about my husband, but I didn't miss the tremendous effort of trying to get him to connect.

When my husband left, he told me that he was tired of disappointing me, and I understood perfectly, because I hated the feeling of being disappointed by him. I started to feel the tiniest kernel of relief that he would no longer be my problem.

In the absence of other relationships, I felt my connection to my own child deepen. Surrounded by other two-parent families, I saw how singular our particular thread was.

I'm certain that all mothers feel an intense and intimate attachment to their children, but what the parenting books never tell you is how knowing your own child is a process that happens over time. In the first two years of her life, my feelings about my daughter had been entangled with how I felt about her father and what was happening to our family. Now it was just the two of us, and we were learning to read each other.

The kiddy pool was our universe writ very small. I watched Emily try to navigate her world as I tried to navigate mine. The toddlers crashed around, bumping, grabbing, laughing, crying, swallowing, and spitting pool water, pushing one another and retreating to their mothers when their plastic diaper covers leaked and their Pampers filled with water and threatened to explode.

Mothers interceded frequently, forcing their children to share their water toys and asking them to please say "please."

I don't like to share and I'm often amazed that we insist that our children do it. Being nice is one thing. It's important to be kind, respectful, and polite. But why should a child give up something that belongs to her, just because someone else wants to take it? Still a toddler, Emily had already given up a lot. Too much, I thought. I whispered to her, "If something is yours, then it belongs to you. You don't have to share it unless you want to." She stood her ground, maintaining a death grip on whatever object she was currently attached to, her feet firmly planted. The other toddlers learned to accommodate this quirk.

It has been my particular fate to raise a child whose temperament is almost the polar opposite of mine. The things that I hold on the surface—every waking thought, word, and emotion—seemed submerged in my little girl. She was quiet and wary. Intense.

When she spoke, she used complete sentences, and her slight English accent and precise articulations often caught me by surprise.

Once, just before our move to the States when I was strolling her through our neighborhood in London, a passerby stopped to admire her as she was lying in her pram. "Oh, what a lovely baby. How old is she?" the woman asked me.

Emily glanced up. Her eyes looked like black buttons.

"I'm eighteen months old," she said.

The woman looked alarmed.

"I know," I said. "Honestly, it's a little scary."

But even the most articulate toddlers can't describe their feelings. Young children cannot ask for what they need the most. They can only try to get it. My daughter and I alternated between clinging to each other and trying to escape each other. When she could no longer stand the sight of me, Emily would retreat to her little tree house bedroom. I would find her lining up her toys in neat rows on her bed, talking to them and ordering them around. She conjured a friend named "Charlie," who kept her company before and after naptime. She invented destinations that she and Charlie would visit.

Without me.

When you're a single parent, you're often lonely, yet seldom alone. There is no backup and no spontaneous escape from parenthood—even for a minute. I had a friend who was a stay-at-home mom who told me that when she got overwhelmed, she would lie in wait for her husband to return from work. The minute he crossed the threshold, she would hand him the baby and go out to a bar, where she would sit and smoke cigarettes and watch basketball on the bar's TV for a couple of hours until she felt better. No single parent has that luxury. Any escape from the kids is the result of intense planning and/or significant expenditure. It is mothering without a net.

I learned to pace myself. I broke down the day into its parts: eating, playing, swimming, resting, reading. I didn't think past noon, and then once noon came, I didn't think past four. When Emily took her afternoon nap during the hottest part of the day, I would train a fan on her and lie down on my bed and stare at the trees outside the window.

In the evenings, I would count the minutes before bedtime, after which I would sit on the couch, talk to my mother on the phone, moon about my failed marriage, and stare at the television before stumbling off to bed. Many nights, I would wake with a start at around 4 A.M. Lying alone in my bed I would watch the gnarly shadows from the trees dance on my ceiling while I replayed the drama and romance of my daughter's birth.

I had become alarmed during my pregnancy when I tried to interest my husband in my impending motherhood, but he didn't seem to want to talk about it. I tried to get him to tell me how he felt about becoming a father, but he wouldn't talk about that, either. His one concession to looming fatherhood was to buy a jokey book by Bill Cosby that he kept on the nightstand but didn't read. He helped to put the crib together, painted and furnished the baby's room, and obsessed over names, but he didn't attend prenatal classes with me and seemed most comfortable viewing our family as Cary Grant might in an old movie—beautifully dressed and from an ironic distance.

The message I got was that in our little family, parent-hood was happening to me, but not necessarily to him.

Late in my pregnancy, I panicked. I could see the little hairline fractures that would later become the fissures lead-ing to our broken home. I confronted him and told him that I was scared about the birth. I said I worried that he wouldn't be there for me when it came time for the baby to be born. "I'm a deadline guy," he reassured me. "You'll see—I'll be fine."

The night I went into labor my husband and I sped through Knightsbridge in a taxi on the way to the hospital.

He held my hand and said, "Just think—the next time we see this place, we'll have our baby with us."

He was right about being a deadline guy. During our daughter's birth, he read to me and whispered to me. When they were administering the epidural he said, "Just think of your favorite place. Pretend that you are rocking in a chair on your mother's porch in Freeville." But that was the last time I remember feeling truly connected to him. After that the rest of our marriage seemed like a long good-bye.

Being a parent, it turns out, isn't about deadlines. It's about the space in between.

In my own bed at the start of my new life, awakened by anxiety, I passed the time waiting to fall back asleep by worrying about bill paying and job hunting and the prospect of going on dates. I wondered if it was my peculiar fate to always be a part of a broken family and wondered how deeply it would wound my daughter not to have a father regularly in her life.

Parents describe the world to their growing children. We are the ones who show and tell them what life is like. Babies scan their mothers' faces for signs of distress. They'll cry when they see it.

I decided that I wanted to be happy. I knew I would feel better if I found a way to make a life for us, and I knew that I would do it on my own.

Parenting is not a process of control but of surrender. I learned this during the dreamy months of our first summer.

My best efforts to build a model family had failed. I led a guy to fatherhood, but I couldn't make him stay.

We are not our best intentions. We are what we do. My husband taught me that.

Now I had to build something out of what was left. Emily and I were two dots, connected by a thread. I decided that whatever strange shape or structure our family assumed—it would never feel broken.

THREE

Ex Marks the Spot

Separating in a Time of Togetherness

OUR NEW HOME in Washington was an apartment in a landmark 1930 art deco building made of pale yellow bricks, situated right next to the National Zoo. The building had once been the grand home of cabinet members and congressmen. Now it was faded, dated, and housed a substantial population of very elderly people, most of whom had lived there for decades. Like many in Washington, the residents of the Kennedy-Warren marked time by presidential administrations; when asked how long they had lived in the building, they would say, "I've been here since Truman," or "We came here during Nixon/Ford."

Many afternoons after coming home from nursery school, Emily would pack her toy stroller with her favorite doll and we would stroll from our apartment to the lobby to get the mail. The spacious lobby was the main gathering place for our elderly neighbors, who would bring their canes and walkers and sit in overstuffed chairs lining the once elegant reception room. They would then spend the bulk of the afternoon yelling across the lobby at one another and harassing Charles, the uniformed doorman who worked the afternoon shift. Our neighbors liked to help Charles do his job. "Delivery!" they'd shout at the first sign of the UPS truck pulling into the circular driveway. "Thank you! I didn't see that gigantic brown truck pull up!" Charles would shout back, then he'd push his cap back on his head, roll his eyes, and walk outside to greet the driver.

Whenever Emily and I entered the lobby, she had to run the gauntlet created by these people, who would shout out greetings and questions as if she were at a White House press conference attended by the grandchild-deprived cast of *Cocoon*.

"What's your dolly's name, Emily?"

"Going to the zoo today?"

"Let me see your pretty dress!"

"Where's your daddy, honey?"

It amazed me how often people would ask my young daughter where her absent father was. Children coming to our home for playdates would check out our apartment with its girly furniture, notice immediately that it was de-

48

void of a male presence, and ask, "Where's your daddy?" Their mothers were equally curious. On the playground they would point a retrieved sippy cup toward Emily. *"Where's her father?"* they would stage-whisper.

Where I might have been tempted to reply to children by filling in the story with wordy explanations about how sometimes mommies and daddies just grow apart and it's no one's fault, Emily would always deliver an elegantly simple answer:

He's in Moscow.

I was astonished that this answer was enough. Even when kids didn't know what "Moscow" was, they never inquired further. Emily didn't know what Moscow was, either, though she had once been there—during a two-week springtime tour when she was a baby. Adults were less easily satisfied. *"Does she see him?"* they'd ask. I'd reply, "Oh yes. Now and then. Well, not that often. It's a long way away, but she sees him a little."

Sometimes at night Emily and I would take her light-up globe off the shelf and I would trace her finger from Washington, DC, across the Atlantic Ocean, skimming over Ireland, pausing at our former home in England, and zigzagging through Europe before finally hovering over Russia. "There it is. Moscow. That's where your daddy is!"

Ex marks the spot.

In the second year of our daughter's life and the last year of our marriage my husband, a television journalist, became Johnny Assignment. Johnny Assignment was the guy they called upon when there was work to be done in Afghanistan. He packed his bag for Islamabad, Brussels, and Prague. He spent Thanksgiving on assignment in Armenia and didn't return home until mid-December. He had only been home for two hours from that particular trip when the office called. He was out enjoying his posttrip ritual—buying a newspaper and *People* magazine—and by the time he came back the company car and driver were waiting for him, idling on the street outside our London flat. He switched suitcases and was gone again. He returned at the end of January.

Sometimes we joined him on the road. As democracy and capitalism swept across Eastern Europe, I found myself holding Emily on my lap on airplanes crowded with entrepreneurs who were rushing into Hungary or the Czech Republic with their briefcases stuffed with contracts and, I imagined, whatever currency was required to bribe local officials. (I carried a bag stuffed with Huggies.) I changed Emily's diaper on the airport floor near the luggage carousel while waiting for our bags in Budapest. Later during that trip, she took her first steps. I took her to the puppet theater in Moscow, and she toddled through Red Square. But I wasn't good at doing family life on the road. Feeding her while she sat strapped into her stroller instead of a high chair, putting her to bed in a portable crib in a hotel room while I watched CNN on mute and waited for him to come back—the limits and loneliness of it became too much. We stayed behind while he kept going.

Occasionally I lost track of where in the world he was, so I took to imagining Johnny Assignment wearing a variety of traditional costumes and hats. When he would call at night, I'd close my eyes and envision him wearing lederhosen with kneesocks and clogs, a peasant blouse, and a green felt Robin Hood hat. I pictured him wearing a caftan, a dishdasha, a Nehru jacket, a fez, and a fedora. I saw him in one of those Soviet-style winter hats made of rabbit fur, like the one I remember seeing Leonid Brezhnev wearing on TV. When he came home from a trip with a photo of himself sporting one of those very same hats and standing next to a donkey in the high desert of Afghanistan, I realized that I had already conjured that exact picture—including the donkey. "Ha! But who's that jackass with the donkey?" I asked him.

When our marriage ended, he headed east toward Russia while we went west toward Freeville. Just before moving day, he told me that he had accepted a long-term assignment in Moscow. I couldn't figure out why he was moving such a great distance when we were also changing continents, but I assumed that he chose Russia because the Moon, Mars, and A Galaxy Far Far Away were already booked. We would be, quite literally, on opposite ends of the Earth.

In the two years since Emily and I had moved to Washington, our lives were starting to fill in. I was finding work during school hours as a freelance researcher, and friendship had begun to eddy into the deepest parts of my loneliness.

I had also stopped crying. Only Emily's baby pictures or the sight of an old couple holding hands on Connecticut Avenue could make me tear up.

In two years of separation Emily had seen her father a handful of times. She knew who he was—we had some photos of him around the apartment and she saw him do reports on television from time to time—and I tried to talk about him freely, though not too frequently. I didn't want to turn him into some sort of mythical daddy creature who Emily could think about but rarely see.

I knew how to reach him but I seldom tried, partly because Emily was too timid to talk on the phone. He called occasionally and let me know whenever he was planning a trip to the States. Three or four times a year he would fly to New York and take the train to DC, stay in a hotel, and visit for a couple of days. Sometimes he took Emily to his hotel and they would swim in the hotel's pool, watch cartoons, and eat room service meals. They seemed to have a very easy, loving, and warm rapport, and I liked seeing the two of them together. Occasionally she stayed overnight with him, and then I would meet them for breakfast the next day. The three of us would walk through the zoo together or do some other touristy thing.

It was a few days before Thanksgiving, five months after his most recent visit, when my ex-husband knocked on the door. I put on my excited face—a mask of joviality that I hoped would obscure my anxiety, but that instead transformed me into a masquerade of phony-happy. I gathered the backpack and the little suitcase on rollers that Emily would take to the airport. Our four-year-old had disappeared into her room, the point farthest from the front door of our apartment.

I thought that we had become adept at separating. I was eager for my little girl to have her father in her life. Unfortunately for all of us, this time she had to leave me in order to do that.

This trip was going to be different. He would be staying with his family in New York over Thanksgiving. He had come to Washington to retrieve Emily and then take her back to New York for a few days. It would be fun. This is what I focused on when discussing it with Emily. They would go to the Macy's Parade on Thanksgiving Day! They would see Santa Claus and the Rockettes and grandparents and cousins!

"Everybody loves New York," I said to her as we packed her suitcase. "That's where Sesame Street is. They have the best pizza and the funniest people, and that's why everybody wants to live there."

Emily was quiet.

"Are you coming too?"

"No. I'm going to stay here for three days and then I'm going to take the train to New York and come and get you and we'll come back together on the train. That sounds fun, doesn't it?"

Her eyes got watery. Blink blink.

"Why don't you pick out three friends to take with

you?" I asked her. We scanned the stuffed animals lined up on the bed. "Oh no—they all want to come!" I scolded her teddy bear for crawling into the suitcase.

"Do you want to know what I'm going to do while you're away?" I asked her. She nodded. I tried to come up with the least enticing activities I could think of.

"I'm going to eat vegetables and vacuum the apartment. Then I'm going to the bank and the post office, and I'm going to drop off the car at the garage."

"Will you take the car to Greg?" (Greg was our mechanic.) "Won't he wonder where I am?" she asked. I pictured her empty car seat.

"I know he'll ask about you. So what should I tell him?"

"You can say that I'm in New York with my dad," she said.

I SCREWED UP my first good-byes with Emily when she started nursery school. When I delivered her to the classroom, her teacher Gay greeted her warmly. "Let's find you a job to do," she said and took Emily by the hand. I lingered by the threshold of the room. Emily looked back, saw me, and ran into my arms. Much clinging ensued. It was as if we were auditioning for a silent movie melodrama; she was being sent to the orphanage, and I was about to be pushed out onto an ice floe. I decided to stick around until she felt better. But she never really felt better while I was sticking around. I watched the more seasoned parents bringing their veteran nursery schoolers into the classroom with a cheerful good-bye and a quick exit. Even the kids who cried tended to stop very quickly once their parent was gone as the teacher swiftly moved them from the parent into the classroom's embrace.

I saw how selfish it was to linger and cling, how it impeded Emily's progress and reflected my own inability to let go of her. The message I needed to convey instead was that it was OK to be apart and that she could trust herself and the people around her. She needed to see that she could live in the world and have experiences without me and to learn that hello follows good-bye and that people do come back.

By age four, we had mastered the nursery school drop-off. She was less sensitive, and I was too. This departure for New York felt loaded, however. I wasn't leaving her. This time she was leaving me.

"Emily, get your stuff because your dad's here . . . ," I called out, singsongy.

I opened the door. He looked exactly the same. He always looked exactly the same. I rarely saw him in person, but I saw him often in my mind's eye—and whenever I looked at our daughter. He had adopted the national costume of the country he was currently visiting and was wearing sneakers, chinos, a suede jacket, and like every other man that particular year, a baseball cap. He had spent the night in a nearby hotel and had a cab waiting to take the two of them to the airport.

He wore roughly the same mask as mine. He was Wink Martindale. I was Kathie Lee Gifford.

"She's feeling a little shy, I think. I'll go get her," I said.

He stood in the doorway.

I went into Emily's room and scooped her up into my arms. Right away I realized that this was a mistake. This sort of transfer called for a businesslike leading by the hand. I felt her arms tighten around my neck. I feared that one of us would not survive this particular embrace.

I carried her out toward the door. Her dad stepped in, stroked her back, and told her how excited he was about the trip. "Where's your suitcase—do you think you'd better get it? We need to get in the taxi and then go to the airport!" He sounded like a game show host. "You've just won a brand-new car!" I half-expected him to gesture over to where Carol Merrill was standing, stroking a side-by-side refrigerator.

I tried the no-nonsense approach.

"OK. Let's stand on your feet and get going. I'll walk you and Daddy down to the lobby."

She held on tighter around my neck. *This is going to leave a mark. I am going to have the world's largest kid-hickey.*

He reached down and picked up Emily's *Beauty and the Beast* backpack and little suitcase. We exchanged glances. He looked completely hapless. I hated that look and the way he tended to wait until I told him what to do. I also hated the fact that I told him what to do. I didn't want to be in charge, now or ever.

"OK. Let's go. Let's just go." Emily was wrapped around me; I could feel her feet lock against the small of my back. Surgically removing her from me would require a team of specialists, including, of course, a shrink. Like many parents, I occasionally pondered which of my mistakes would land our daughter in therapy. Look no further—we have a winner!

Our only option was for her father to literally peel her away from me and carry her away by force. This seemed more a kidnapping than a fun parental visitation featuring Santa Claus and the Rockettes—and we would all surely suffer. Emily had already demonstrated the unfortunate combination of an elephantine memory and an unforgiving nature. She had still not forgiven her aunt Rachel for a two-day stint of babysitting earlier that year, during which time she rode a pink bike with training wheels, was spoiled silly by her older cousin, stayed up past her bedtime, and ate her lunch off a TV tray while watching soap operas. If she found *that* unforgivable, how was this going over?

We boarded the elevator. Emily was snuffling and sniffling. I felt the beginning of a sob rise up through her body; my solar plexus was like a radio receiver, feeling her emotions rocketing into my own gut as we walked through the lobby and toward the entrance of the building. Charles, on duty that day, looked at us and shook his head. He opened the passenger door of the taxi. I wasn't wearing any shoes. I attempted to unpeel one of Emily's fingers from the back of my neck, but she tightened.

"I'm coming to the airport with you. OK, now. I'll ride along with you," I said. I wondered, Would they allow a barefoot mother with no ID to board the aircraft? Would the flight attendant serve me enough alcohol to render this scene forgettable? Would my ex-husband's girlfriend be joining them in New York on this particular visit? If so, what would they ask Emily to call her? His family had a WASPy tendency to adopt unfortunate nicknames. Emily's grandparents had asked their grandchildren to call them Ta Ta and Num Num. Would my poor little girl have to refer to her daddy's girlfriend as "Kiki" or "Bun-Bun"? Could I refer to her as "Nitwit" and get away with it?

The taxi driver looked at us through the rearview mirror. Emily's face was buried in my clavicle. She was doing a low, guttural motor rev, like a moped in need of an oil change. Nobody said anything.

The drive to National Airport took about fifteen minutes. I pointed out our favorite sights as we passed them. "Look—there's the Washington Monument! Oh—I can see some of the planes now! They look very small up in the sky! There's the Jefferson Memorial!" I stroked her back and murmured into her ear, "Everything's going to be all right, honey. You'll see. And I'll come and get you in three days, just like we talked about." Her panic softened into something that felt like sadness. I felt it in my joints.

We pulled into the departure area outside the terminal, and my ex got out of the taxi and walked around to our side. He opened the door and quietly grasped Emily under her arms. I felt her legs unlock as she transferred her cling from me to him. Nobody asked anybody to say good-bye. Nobody waved bye-bye.

He gave the driver $40. "Can you take her back?" he asked, nodding to me. The driver said yes. My ex looked my way. "Sorry," he mouthed. I winced.

I settled back into the seat and sniffed. The driver looked at me again in the rearview mirror. He was Egyptian, I guessed. I glanced at his license hanging from the sun visor and it said NASIR.

"Oh my. My my. That is very sad," he said. He reached over to the passenger side and pulled out a box of Kleenex and handed the box back to me.

"Oh well." I so often wanted to be jaunty and yet I so seldom was. I took out a tissue and blew my nose.

"Give me back the box, OK?"

I gave it back to him.

"I mean, I've seen some sad things and that is definitely sad," he said. He took out a tissue and blew his nose on it. "I'm crying here myself."

I said a prayer to the Egyptian sun god Ra for this man to please ignore me. I pictured Emily walking through the metal detector and wondered what I would do while she was gone. No doubt my fun kidless activities would mainly involve me sitting alone in a movie theater, buried in a bucket of popcorn.

The driver put the taxi into gear and started to pull away.

"You know, it is what it is. This has to happen sometimes

and you can't do anything about it. You just have to go along with it," he said, expressing a fatalism unfamiliar to my ears.

"Maybe, but I don't have to like it." I leaned forward and helped myself to another tissue, hanging my head through the gap in his Plexiglas barrier. We were a team now, he and I. Perhaps we could teach a "Love 'em and Leave 'em" seminar together at the Learning Annex.

"Well, even if you don't like it, you must pretend that you do. It's for the girl's sake. If you don't want her to go, then she'll know it and she won't want to go, just like this here." Yes. God forbid that Emily might not want to be force-marched onto planes and trains in order to spend time with Ta Ta, Num Num, the Rockettes, and Santa Claus. And Nitwit.

And Papa.

I HAD MY own singular experience with postdivorce visitation in 1974, when my sisters and I spent a weekend visiting our father. He had settled in a small town in the far-north region of New York State known as the North Country with Joan, the truck stop waitress who would become the second of his five wives. I don't know how the visit was arranged—I never remember my father being in touch after he left—but the summer after his departure our mother told us that he would be coming to Freeville to pick us up for the weekend. I was thirteen. My sisters were fifteen and sixteen. My brother had been spared this visit by hitchhiking his way through Scandinavia with a friend.

Dad drove into the driveway in one of his salvaged vehicles. We each had a paper bag with our stuff in it. Mom assured us that everything would be fine. It might even be fun! She walked us out to his car and gave me a tight hug. We exchanged awkward greetings with Dad, who stubbed out his cigarette in the driveway and said, "Well, let's go."

We got into the car; my sisters muscled me out of the backseat, forcing me to sit in front. Dad talked the whole way, blabbing and bragging about the fascinating countryside in the North Country. He quoted its spectacular snowfall statistics and said that he had his eye on a little farm up near Lowville, where he and Joan lived.

We arrived at dusk. Joan's house was set back from the road in the trees. The Black River, which was in fact black, stagnant, and gloomy (Dad said its deep color was caused by the excessive amount of tannin from the trees lining the bank), was just across the road.

Joan was a bruiser wearing a waitress uniform. She had a prized collection of special-edition Jim Beam bottles, the kind you see displayed in the window of the liquor store. One was shaped like Elvis's head. Another looked like a bear. Otherwise, the place was dark, spartan, and sheathed in old linoleum. Joan had a number of children. Two were currently in juvie and the rest had scattered—perhaps away visiting their own fathers (we never met any of them). There was little evidence of her kids in the house.

Joan smoked and stroked our father's arm during dinner. My sisters and I said we were tired and went up the creaky stairs to where we would sleep—an empty bedroom with a linoleum floor. We were given blankets and pillows and slept close together on the floor. "I'm going to get me one of them bottle heads!" I whispered to Rachel, and she laughed. I lay awake for a long time that night, worried about the fact that I didn't know where the light switch was in the room, in case one of Joan's cigarettes set the plastic curtains on fire and we had to get out.

Dad spent the next day driving us around, pointing out various rock outcroppings and other unusual features of the countryside, which he found fascinating. He asked us a few questions about school, but it was hard keeping a conversation going, so he babbled along, peppering his monologue with the sorts of made-up factoids and statistics that were his specialty. We ate lunch at the highway diner where Joan worked, and she assumed a prideful sort of ownership as she brought our food. If I thought about Joan I would loathe her, and yet somehow I knew that she would be of little consequence to me. I decided that I would take a stand on Joan only if forced. I wondered why Mom had let us come and worried that Dad would somehow make us visit more often. If necessary, I would get myself enrolled in some sort of residential program that would make future visits impossible. Not juvie, so much, but maybe boarding school. I wondered what Mom was doing with all of her free time and pictured her reading a book, which is what she did whenever she was stuck waiting for us at school or after track meets, basketball games, or band practice. Maybe she was sick of us and liked being by herself.

My sisters and I spent one more suppertime at Joan's house, quietly eating while the night closed in on us—the dark creeping through the trees, up Joan's long driveway and into her linoleum kitchen. Dad gassed on and Joan chain-smoked and stroked his arm. He was working construction building a prison over near Watertown. He'd do that until he started farming again, he said. He'd left a perfectly good farm and family already. Why do that again? I wondered.

I couldn't wait to get home. We were quiet in the car as Dad drove us south, and for the first time all weekend, he was subdued too. Compared to Lowville, Freeville seemed light, colorful, and airy. I had never been to Miami, but surely this is what it felt like down south. Warm and summery.

Dad dropped us off in the driveway next to our old and empty barn and told us, "Tell your mother I said hi." "Thanks, Dad—that was really interesting!" I said as I grabbed my paper bag and turned toward our house. I noticed the colorful petunias tumbling and climbing in one of Mom's many flower beds.

We went into the house. Mom was standing on a chair,

painting the trim of our living room. The large room looked completely different from when we had left, just two days before. She had painted the walls and trim and rearranged the furniture.

She shyly said hello to us and laughed about the room. "I didn't have much to do while you were gone," she said.

She was holding a paintbrush. "Well, put your stuff away and I'll start supper," she said. I felt like I had been away for two weeks, and the altered room made me feel like a visitor.

Mom never asked us pointed questions, but during supper I couldn't stand it anymore and spilled the beans. I described the Jim Beam bottle collection, and then my sisters weighed in with the creepy dark house and the kids in juvie, and Dad's incessant bravado. Finally, I said, "And Joan—whoa. She's seriously a battle-axe. No kidding, Mom. Like a professional wrestler."

My mother let out a quick breath. I didn't realize until then that she had been holding so much in. "It can't be that bad," she said.

"It is that bad," we said, laughing. "Don't make us go there again."

"OK," she said. "You're off the hook."

I realized for the first time how hard this had been on our mother. Like most kids, I had taken our attachment for granted. I knew I needed her, but did she need me? I'd simply never thought about it. Later she confessed that she was worried that we would want to be with our father and that she would lose us to him. But still—she had to let us go. Her fears and feelings were immaterial.

NASIR THE CABBIE had a point—and one that none of my intimates had dared make to me. Sometimes you have to pretend that it's easy to let go. The only reason to do this is to make life easier for someone else. There are times when the right thing is to willingly board the ice floe. I could try to do that.

Nasir pulled the cab into the circular drive in front of the building. On Saturday mornings, those few residents who had children tended to bring them out onto the front lawn to play. The kids toddled and pecked like a flock of chickens let out into the barnyard. Charles watched benignly over them and was usually available to keep an eye out if you had to dash back into the apartment for a forgotten snack or toy. Emily was often part of this little gang of babies and toddlers who would careen around on the grass, pushing their miniature strollers or playing with their plastic golf clubs. On this warm fall morning, some of the pint-size regulars were there, along with their parents distractedly nursing that morning's third cup of coffee. I tried not to look at the kids, though I observed bitterly that it would have been nice if Emily could have spent the morning pushing her toy stroller rather than a suitcase. I gingerly got out of the cab, feeling the pavement under my bare feet and realizing for the first time that I also wasn't wearing a bra.

Nasir proffered a ten-dollar bill out the window. "He gave me too much," he said.

"Oh no. Keep it," I told him. "You've definitely earned it."

I reached into the cab, grabbed one more tissue for the road, and went inside.

When I got upstairs to our apartment, its emptiness hit me like a wave. The phone rang. It was my ex. "I just want you to know that everything is fine; we're about to board now. Emily—hey; do you want to say hi? Let me lift her up." I heard the airport announcements blaring and the sound of the pay phone's receiver fumbling as he passed it to Emily. I had never heard my daughter's voice on the phone before—I had only experienced her as I thought I should—in person.

"Hi, Mommy!" she said.

"Hi, honey. Are you ready to go? Are you going to have fun?"

"Yes."

"And when will I come get you?"

"In three days."

"That's right; in three days."

FOUR

Nothing's Too Much Trouble

O N EASTER SUNDAY when Emily was in first grade, Rachel and I walked through Freeville, talking, as we frequently do, about what should happen next. We are schemers, she and I, and have spent a lifetime trading ideas. There was a time during our childhood when our discussions focused on how to leave home, but it turns out we were no match for our hometown's pull. After graduate school, Rachel had never managed to live more than ten miles away from Freeville—and now we talked about how I could come at least partway back too.

Rachel and I stopped in the middle of Union Street, right about in the spot where a painted yellow line would run down the street if it had a lane divider, which it does not. A few local house cats were lounging in the middle of the street, lying on the warm blacktop and switching their tails. The street was quiet and without traffic, as usual.

"How about that one?" Rachel asked. She was pointing straight across the intersection with Main Street at a small house fronted by a FOR SALE sign. The sign had popped one of its fasteners and was dangling and swinging in the sharp spring breeze like a man in trouble.

"Eeeew," I blurted out.

The house was tall and narrow. A cinder block chimney ran up its front. Two small casement windows poked through the upper floor like bloodshot eyes; a bowfronted and crookedly placed faux bay window stretched across part of the bottom floor. The house looked like a child's drawing of a house if the child had no talent and was in a hurry. It was the house equivalent of a guy who had gone on a bender and been kicked out of rehab. If this house had parents, they would have disowned it and moved to Buffalo, leaving no forwarding address. Homely in the extreme, it had languished for two years in the dregs of the perennially pillow-soft local housing market.

The little house stood next to the far more handsome home where my aunt Millie now lived, which was built by my great-grandfather in 1886 and had been occupied by family members ever since. A generation ago, the homely house that was now for sale had also been in our family for a time. When I was a very young child, my great aunt Jane had lived there, but after her death it had passed through several neglectful and abusive owners, like an unlucky character in an Edith Wharton novel.

Not only was this house *not* the house of my dreams, but I'd also ridden past it on my bike forty-seven times a day during the entirety of my childhood and had never even really looked at it.

However, this house cost $58,000, so I decided to buy it.

FOR MUCH OF my life I have been afflicted with material and personal desires that some members of my family might decry as "fancy pants." Owning a second home fit into the version of myself I'd created during childhood, when my fantasy life involved going to the barn and placing hay bales in a depressingly *Hee Haw* approximation of Johnny Carson's set and pretending that I was both the host and the most fascinating guest of the legendary late-night talk show. With no specific notion about how I would get there, I knew that I was destined to live in New York City (a place I had seen only in the movies), with a second home in a compatible setting. For part of the year, I would live in a place like Kykuit.

When I was a kid and Nelson Rockefeller was the flamboyant, bell-bottomed governor of New York State, I read about Kykuit in *Life* magazine. Kykuit was where Governor Rockefeller went when he needed to clear his head. Situated on two hundred acres in the Hudson Valley, the grand estate of the Rockefeller family featured art galleries, fireplaces big enough to walk into, sculpture gardens, terraced flower beds, Hudson River views, a coach house filled with classic automobiles, guest quarters, and a structure delightfully called the Temple of Aphrodite.

In my imaginings, I would marry a distant Rockefeller cousin, preferably one who wasn't too messed up and who looked somewhat like Donny Osmond, and we would have use of the Rockefeller estate as a second home. We wouldn't even need to stay in the main house; we'd be perfectly happy in one of the guest cottages. My vision of life as a grown-up was very specific on this score. I would live at Kykuit.

I left Freeville at seventeen, but my leave-taking didn't seem to take. I always seemed to travel in the same direction, even when I didn't specifically intend to—my personal compass was permanently set toward home.

During college in Washington, I could force my homesickness into long remissions, but then it would surface and I'd board a Greyhound bus and make it halfway home from DC to Scranton, Pennsylvania, where my mother would drive three hours to fetch me. My mother is the person for whom the phrase "nothing is too much trouble" was coined. Since she was a homebody herself who likes to travel but hates to be away, I never had to explain my impulses to her.

"So, what's going on this weekend in Freeville?" I'd ask excitedly as I got into her brown Plymouth Duster.

"Nothing. Not a damn thing," she'd say.

"Well, it's a good thing I came home because I'd hate to miss that."

In college, I became friendly with people who came from places like Greenwich, Winnetka, and Shaker Heights—hometowns that, unlike mine, needed no further introduction. Their childhoods, like their houses, sounded expansive, complicated, and dreamy. They lost their virginity in their pool cabanas and were given cars for their sixteenth birthdays.

My college friend John was rumored to come from a Connecticut branch of the Kennedy family tree, though I tried not to hold his wealth and connections against him as I marveled at his Ultra Brite smile and carefully placed neck-knotted sweater. Just before my first spring break from college, John asked if I'd like to "go in on" a sailboat trip he was putting together with other friends. The group would sail in the Caribbean over the break. The eventual destination would be a vacation place his family had in Barbados.

While I assumed that the contrast between our upbringings was obvious, and while I didn't want to put too fine a point on it, the whole time that John was talking to me about the trip, I was thinking about the time my father killed a rabbit and we ate it. (We didn't eat it because we had to, but more because we could.) "Oh, I don't think I could afford the sailing thing," I said, and then John winked knowingly at me and replied, "Why don't you just get the 'rents to pay for it?"

I was still learning the preppy vernacular but quickly figured out that 'rents were PArents. And as I hadn't seen my own pa in five years and didn't quite know where he was currently located, I didn't think there was much like-lihood that he'd spring for a sailing trip.

My new circle of college friends had many things to envy. They were good-looking, smart, and had shiny hair. They could make jokes using their high school Latin. They wore sherbet-colored corduroys printed with ducks, whales, and anchors and knew how to turn up the collars on their polo shirts so they were stiff in the back and winglike in the front.

The lives of most of my colleagues seemed stocked with options. When it was time to go home for a visit, they had a choice. This home or that? Beach or mountains, Florida or Maine? My eventual college boyfriend, who became my eventual husband, grew up in New York City with a second family home in the Hamptons, which he referred to, quaintly, as "the country." As in, "Let's go out to the country to see the 'rents." This country life, located off a boutique-crowded street and complete with membership to an exclusive beach club and another even more restrictive tennis club, seemed less "country" and more an extension of Mad-ison Avenue.

Unfortunately for me, the more I was exposed to the lifestyle to which I had aspired for most of my life, the less I seemed to want it. When my husband and I visited his fam-ily in their beautiful Hamptons home, I was hyperaware of my many deficits. I wasn't tall enough, well dressed enough, or pretty in ways that are noticeable to people who notice these things. I talked too much, and I didn't know how to talk about the things they talked about: real estate, un-solved high-society murders, movie star sightings, and sail-ing. I played the wrong sports (softball instead of tennis). I put my feet up on the coffee table and got accidentally drunk and laughed too loudly during the cocktail hour. Also, I sweat. And it's not the dewy kind of sweat, but the "I've Been Working on the Railroad" underarm-stains-the-size-of-the-Bronx kind. When my marriage ended, my only comfort was in knowing that I'd likely never have to brave life in "the country" again.

IN RETROSPECT, I realize that I didn't exactly inspect my little house in Freeville carefully before buying it, though Emily and I went through it together and noticed that cer-tain houselike elements, such as doors, a staircase, toilet, and sinks, were in fact present. The official building inspector said that the house was surprisingly "solid" for a structure of its age (it was built in 1900) and that, aside from the fact that the porch seemed to be listing toward the driveway and threatened to detach from the rest of the house, the house itself was basically sound. The structure, which measured roughly nine hundred square feet upstairs and down, con-sisted of one main room with a galley kitchen and bathroom downstairs, and three small bedrooms and a half-bathroom upstairs. The current owners, two guys who bought the place when they were students at the local community col-lege, had gutted the house and reassembled it in the 1980s.

Their handiwork reflected what I imagined to be the taste and abilities of two twenty-year-olds who had taken but not necessarily passed shop class in high school.

The house's "negatives" were mainly cosmetic. The student/owners had done all of the work themselves, using materials that I surmised may have fallen off of a truck headed through town on its way to Atlantic City. Flesh-colored, nylon shag carpeting two inches deep blanketed almost every floor surface except for the kitchen and bathroom—including the staircase leading to the (fully carpeted) bedrooms and half-bath upstairs. Unfortunately the relatively shallow depth of the hundred-year-old stair risers covered with the thick shag reduced the actual surface area of each individual step by four inches or so. This meant that the steps were no longer secure resting places for one's foot but had become slippery toeholds, turning the staircase itself into a steep toboggan run of fear. During our first walk-through, the real estate agent, Emily, and I each lost our footing in turn, sliding down the entire length of the staircase—thumping onto each successive step and picking up speed while sparking code-red levels of static electricity until landing with a thud on the hard pink ceramic tile that had been glued to the floor at the base of the stairs.

"I think those stairs are oak!" the agent said, rubbing his backside.

The owners had tried to class up the place by installing Victorian-esque ceiling fans on as many ceilings as would hold them. In the main downstairs room, this resulted in a mere case of bordello ugliness, but upstairs—where the ceilings were several inches lower and the rooms several feet smaller than even those in a normal-size house—the ceiling fans seemed less cooling devices than instruments of torture. Turning a fan on in an eight-by-ten-foot bedroom, I felt myself flinching, ducking, and hankering to confess to crimes I hadn't committed with each pass of a plastic blade as it skimmed, menacingly, inches over my head. "Of course, when you're lying down in bed, you're not going to notice that. That's a nice little breeze when you think about it," the agent said. I tried not to think about it.

The kitchen of the house shared its floor space with a bathroom across the back of the structure. There was pink tile on the floor, and dark oaklike laminate cupboards lined the walls, supplemented by a beige Formica countertop. Even though the kitchen was already tiny, the owners had evidently decided to emphasize its coziness by dropping the ceiling and hiding their plumbing and electrical handiwork behind a deep soffit, which they had fashioned from nailed-together wallboard. Here the student/builders had breached the dangerous nexus of water + electricity; I shuddered to think of what was behind the flimsy false wall space. The walls and ceiling were painted. "What do you call that color?" I asked the real estate agent. "Tan. Or brown. No, tan," he said.

"Everything is, as far as I know, built to code," he added, helpfully.

Glancing out of the kitchen window, I could see the small shady backyard blanketed with patches of weeds. The yard ended abruptly where it fell off in a steep bank leading down to Fall Creek, which flowed just beyond. I couldn't see the creek from the window, but I could feel it.

I would own waterfront property.

My Kykuit.

I said good-bye to the real estate agent, and after he locked the house and drove away, Emily and I sat together on the porch step, looking out onto the traffic on Main Street. I explained to Emily that if we bought the house, we would have a place of our own to stay in when we visited, but that we'd still live in Washington most of the time.

"So, kid, do you think we should get this house?" I asked her.

She looked around, thinking. "Could I paint my room blue?" she asked.

I said that she could.

"Would we get furniture?"

"We'll find some somewhere," I said.

My aunt Millie, our new next-door neighbor, drove by and waved. "Hel-l-o-o-o!"

The day of the closing, my mother, aunts Millie and Lena, Uncle Harvey, and cousins Nancy and Lorraine wandered by the house. Because of its position on Main Street, each family member could legitimately claim to have been accidentally passing by when she saw Emily and me standing with the real estate agent on the front lawn. My family members decided to hang out on the front porch until we had finished our business with the agent. Everybody offered an opinion on what I should do with the place: it could stand a new paint job and wouldn't it be great to paint it "peach" or "shrimp"? The porch railing was very strange, didn't I think? Hopefully I would choose to cut down that hideous birch tree in front because everybody knows that birch trees belong in shopping malls and industrial parks. Maple is the way to go. There is a "rabbit problem" on Main Street—did anyone think to tell me?

My family members clumped themselves together on the front porch, and I took a picture of them. Then they formed a little cluster in front of the front door and waited patiently to be let in. With some ceremony, the agent handed over the keys to the place. I excused my way through the small crowd and opened the screen door to unlock the front door to my new home—and the screen door promptly came off its hinges and clattered onto the porch. I was left holding the doorknob.

"You can fix that; a couple of screws and you can pop that right back in!" the agent said and quickly got into his car.

Emily and I didn't get to spend our first night in our new home until two months after its purchase. Halloween fell on a weekend that year, so we left Washington very early on Halloween morning and drove north, arriving in Freeville just as dusk was starting to envelop the village. The first hints of the deep cold of the winter to come had pulled most of the leaves off the trees; they swirled in cyclones along Main Street. Freeville has a sort of Sleepy Hollow quality in the fall as the corn in the surrounding fields goes golden and then breaks off in brittle bonelike stalks and the trees gradually go bare, exposing their skeletons to the night sky. The residents treat Halloween like a major holiday and go a little haywire, decorating their houses with paper skeletons, jack-o'-lanterns, and colored lights strung from the trees.

Down Main Street, I could see that my neighbor Bill had, as usual, prepared for the night by digging a fresh grave in his front yard; it was topped with a crooked R.I.P. headstone. Every year on Halloween night when trick-or-treaters knocked on his door, they were greeted with the loud and ghastly howling of Bill's *Hounds of Hell* CD emanating from deep within the house. Once that had sunk in, Bill would whip open the door, looking like Jack Nicholson in *The Shining*. His costume was a checked flannel shirt with suspenders holding up his jeans—he made up his face with deep black circles under his eyes and traces of fake blood. He was carrying an axe.

"Has anybody seen my wife?" he would ask, menacingly, while gesturing with his axe toward the headstone in his yard. Bill's act, with its subtle movie allusions and outright fright factor, may have been intended for a more mature audience; it scared the living daylights out of the average five-year-old trick-or-treater. They had a tendency to scream, drop their candy, and run to the next house while Bill chased after them, apologizing.

Once inside our new house, I turned on the heat, saying a little prayer to the God of the Basement that the furnace worked. I didn't want to get cocky, but I also layered a hope on top of the prayer—that we wouldn't blow up in a fireball caused by a gas leak. I didn't have a couch, so as I waited for the heat to come up I leaned on the sill of the world's ugliest faux bay window and looked onto the street.

In my few weeks of home ownership, I had learned that every single thing having to do with my house seemed to cost $1,000. No matter how large or small the job was, the price was always $1,000. Replacing the screen door that flew off in my hands on the first day? $1,000. Affixing the porch to the house? $1,000. At that rate, it would be at least twenty years before the house was even average-ugly. I tried not to care and then I decided not to care, but I cared anyway. I couldn't help it. I was tired from the long drive from DC and wondered if it was wise to tie myself to a second home when I didn't own a first home. I wondered when I would get my comeuppance for being so fancy pants.

Emily carefully scaled the danger-stairs and went into her empty and echoey bedroom to put on her costume. Every year my sister Anne made Emily's Halloween costume and gave it to her as a birthday present. This year she was Snow White; Emily had been excitedly slipping into her room and emerging in her costume every day after school for the past two weeks. I stood in the darkening house, waiting for my girl to become a Disney character.

Main Street was starting to get crowded with little Power Rangers and princesses. I had planned to turn off the porch light in order to avoid handing out candy, but it turned out that the porch light didn't work anyway ($1,000), so I didn't have to worry about it. After trick-or-treating, Emily and I were going to sit on my cousin Jan's porch with my mother and aunts to count our candy and watch the passing parade as the younger kids went on home and the older kids started to filter out into the night.

I've always been inspired by the spookiness of Halloween and have a weakness for tall tales, legends, and fright lies of all kinds. When my nieces and nephews were young, I'd tell them stories of bears and wolverines run amok, escaped convicts, haunted toolsheds, headless milkmaids, hook man, Peg-Leg Pete, and the monster of Fall Creek. In the summer, when Railey had sleepovers to celebrate her July birthday and the girls brought their sleeping bags to a tent in her yard, I'd swing by to say happy birthday and say, "You're still planning on sleeping out? Oh, I guess you didn't see the newspaper today? Well, it's nothing to worry about, I'm sure. Don't give it another thought." Railey, who was quite used to the "Tall Tales and Legends" portion of my act, would roll her eyes, but there was usually a girl who would take the bait. "What? What's in the newspaper?"

"Oh, it's nothing, I'm sure they caught him by now."

"Caught? Caught who?"

"Oh, you really don't know? Well, they had a breakout over at the Auburn State Prison, but don't worry about it. They caught everybody. Well, almost everybody. There's just one more guy out there." I'd act casual.

Railey would sigh and say in a bored voice, "Oh no. Don't tell me the guy had a hook for a hand, Auntie Amy."

"Oh, then you *did* hear? As a matter of fact, he *does* have a hook for a hand, and I know that he grew up around here, but I don't want you girls to get nervous about it. I'm sorry I even mentioned it. Hey—have fun tonight!"

The previous summer Emily had come with me as I snuck over to Railey's house after dark and scratched on the outside of the tent. This was an integral physical manifestation of the hook man story. We heard a little voice inside: "Hey you guys, you guys, shut up! Did you hear something?"

Much screaming ensued.

Kids didn't seem to want to be scared anymore on Halloween. Emily's elementary school had banned any costumes that they deemed to be "frightening," and so the school costume parade that year was a stream of frisky Bill Clintons and naughty Monica Lewinskys—and one little boy who dressed up as a Secret Service agent, complete with the blue blazer, rep tie, and earpiece.

I hoped that Emily would be granted at least one Halloween night during her own childhood where she would go off on her own, away from my clutching hand. I wanted her to be in a place where she knew that she was safe enough to let herself get good and scared.

"Honey, you better hurry up, it's starting to get really dark!" I called out. Emily said that she was coming right down. I heard an upstairs door open.

"Don't forget to be careful on the st—!" I called out, but it was too late. She had already slipped off the first step and was careening down on her bottom, a pint-size Snow White throwing off static sparks in a not-quite-enchanted cottage.

I caught her at the base of the stairs. "Oh God, are you OK?" I asked. I checked her quickly for injuries—as far as I could tell, she only had a little carpet burn. She wasn't crying or about to cry; mainly she looked mad as hell. Suddenly I felt a little sorry for my neighbor Bill. I had a feeling that this was the year that Snow White might kick his ass.

I smoothed down Emily's blue and yellow gown. "OK then, let's say that was the 'trick.' Now we have to get some treats. We have some people to see. And some ghosts to see. Who-o-o-o-o-o . . ." I made the universal sound for a haunting, made popular by Abbott and Costello movies and Scooby-Doo. She shot me a look. I thought I saw little bolts of lightning flash in her coal black eyes.

We walked out the front door of our very own house and stood on our own porch. I had the house keys with me. Should I lock? I pondered my options. Maybe vandals would toilet paper the inside of the house or steal my—what? I didn't have anything. If I was lucky, someone would come in and steal the rest of the carpet. If I was really lucky they'd have their tools with them and take the kitchen cabinetry.

We stepped out onto the sidewalk. The wind came up and the branches overhead clacked together. A whisper of a shiver ran up my spine.

"Did you feel that?" I asked Emily.

"Feel what?" she said.

"I guess it wasn't anything," I said.

"Are you trying to kid me again about the guy with a hook for his hand?" she asked, skeptically.

"Shut up and hold my hook, I mean my hand," I said—and she did.

FIVE

Making Peanut Jesus

*Finding God in the Community
of Faith and Casseroles*

WHEN I LAST saw him, Peanut Jesus was lying swaddled in a teeny tiny piece of paper towel, resting sweetly in his cardboard manger. I turned my back for a minute in order to stop a covey of boys from putting together a tabletop football game pitting the Wise Men against Joseph and Mary.

I admit that what happened next is something I probably should have anticipated. In my five years of teaching Sunday school to eight- and nine-year-olds at our church in Washington, I had already faced an ark full of preadolescent shenanigans, many having to do with our craft projects and the holy family. I trained myself in the art of the "teachable moment," even at one point uttering the words "Yes, Stuart, that's right. The Virgin Mary does have nipples. Class? Why does the Virgin Mary have nipples? Anyone? Because she was a woman. And she was a mom too. Does anyone know whose mom she was? No?"

After my little Aristotelian monologue, delivered to the mostly smirking and freshly scrubbed faces of my prosperous little charges, I pretty much wanted to run screaming into the street, hail a cab, and go to the nearest bar, until I realized that it was ten-fifteen on a Sunday morning, and if I was lucky enough to find anything open, it would most likely be crowded with Sunday school rejects such as myself—and the last thing I wanted at such a moment was to be in proximity to people who shared my predicament and had been driven to drink by a room full of second graders.

My class of around fifteen kids, which convened after the 9 A.M. service, trooped over to the education building while their parents cruised out to have coffee or a quick brunch at a café. Our weekly ninety-minute sessions were a blur of snacks, stories, simple prayers, and crafts. I liked sending the kids home with something we had made together and got pretty good at thinking up new ways to illustrate the Bible stories we were reading in class. Old Testament–wise, my class and I could knock out individual milk-carton chariots driven by clothespin Philistines in about half an hour. Our Popsicle-stick Ark of the Covenant took two sessions, but only because the glue needed to dry.

My crafty crowning glory, however, was the cereal-box crèche.

This elaborate homemade Nativity scene featured a stable made of a cut-up cereal box populated with cotton ball sheep, cardboard camels, and the holy family, which we made from toilet paper rolls. The star of the cereal-box crèche was Baby Jesus—a peanut still in its shell, swaddled in a tiny piece of paper towel and laid in a cardboard manger.

My class of kids happily participated in the manufacturing of our crèches, cutting, gluing, and excitedly talking about Christmas. We assembled our individual Nativity scenes and reviewed the miraculous story of the birth of Baby Jesus. Then they drifted into their favorite classroom activity, which was to goof around.

While my back was turned, I heard the familiar crack of a peanut shell. The faintest whiff of peanut essence escaped into the atmosphere, like a tiny puff of organic life being released into the stale air of our basement classroom. By the time I turned around, Peanut Jesus' manger was empty. I knelt down, face-to-face with Wyatt West. He was wearing his usual Sunday school outfit—a tiny pair of chinos and a Brooks Brothers navy blue blazer over a light blue oxford shirt. He had a little clip-on necktie. Like many of the boys in my class, Wyatt always looked to me like a miniature congressman on a constituent visit. He was holding two empty peanut shell halves, and looked blankly at me and said, "Wha . . . ?" A small fleck of peanut skin dangled at the corner of his mouth.

"Did you just eat Peanut Jesus?" I asked him.

"That was Jesus?" he said. "I thought that was Joseph."

I decided to ignore the implication that it was somehow all right to eat Peanut Joseph and cut right to the chase.

"No. Joseph is the dad. Class? Who is Joseph?"

I picked up Joseph. His body was made from a toilet paper roll, which we had glued fabric onto and accented with pieces of yarn. Joseph's eyes were pinto beans and his mouth a piece of macaroni. We used little cardboard flaps to make his flipperlike hands and feet.

"This, my friends, is Joseph," I said. I held Joseph aloft. He looked exactly like a toilet roll in drag. RuPaul, by way of Charmin.

Later, on our way home in the car, I reviewed the events of the morning and asked Emily, as I often did, where I had gone wrong. She was a diligent and cooperative fifth grader who didn't have me for a teacher and so could rattle off all the books of the Old and New Testament in thirty-six seconds. I was hoping she would have the perspective I lacked on my class of primary schoolers. "Mom, second grade kids are jerks. Especially second grade boys. They're total spazzes too. And they have potty mouths. Have you listened to the way they talk? Honestly, sometimes I don't know why you bother."

"Thanks," I said. "That was very helpful."

While I was aware that other Sunday school classes at our church's efficiently run education program seemed to impart actual information, my own class of kids retained startlingly little. Sometimes I wondered why they kept coming, week after week, until I realized that most second graders don't exactly have control over their own schedules. Like Emily, these kids came to church because that's what they did on Sundays. It was like soccer practice, ballet, or Little League. They showed up because their parents drove them there.

The following week, I took my concerns to the rector of our church, Reverend Kenworthy. "The kids—I don't know. I don't know if they are getting much out of what I'm doing."

"You're there. You're there every week, and this is your ministry," he said. Like a wise person who answers a question with a question, he dodged my concerns by praising my intentions. But ministry? I didn't think so.

I started teaching Sunday school when Emily was in kindergarten, soon after we started attending Christ Episcopal Church in the fanciest part of swanky Georgetown. I wanted a place for the two of us to go on Sunday mornings, which for me have always felt like a yawning, mournful void—a time when I feel overly homesick and sorry for myself, a time that I only know how to fill with church. The church I chose was fairly high-church Episcopalian, its pretty Gothic interior burnished with the scent of a hundred years' worth of incense. I had attended this same church occasionally when I was a student at Georgetown, whenever I needed a Protestant refuge from the Catholicism of my college.

Famously, some scenes from *The Exorcist* were shot in the church's small side garden. Some mornings, while lingering in the garden during the coffee hour, I pictured Jason Miller, brooding and intense, keeping Satan at bay and surrounded by a film crew.

I grew up in a churchy, if not overtly religious, home, and attending church is one childhood habit I've never seen fit to break. The only years when I didn't attend services regularly were when my husband and I lived in New York City together during the mid-1980s. Then, our Sundays were fully committed to the official New York religious devotions of reading the Sunday *Times* and buying things. Once we moved to London and my husband's job removed him from the Sunday equation, I started occasionally attending church again, always on my own—popping into a small Anglican church on the pretty square across from our apartment.

Emily's first Christmas Eve was spent in a Snugli strapped to me as I stood in the back of the sanctuary of the small church on our London square, sobbing quietly with loneliness (my husband was away) as I followed the candlelight service and wondered what my family was doing half a world away in Freeville. She was two months old and her family hadn't yet met her.

I wanted Emily to know God. I thought I could make the introduction and perhaps stick around for a while to see if these two strangers struck up a cordial conversation. I was like an ambitious hostess at a cocktail party—I didn't want to force a relationship, but once the two started to talk, I would quietly disappear and hope it took.

Later in January during Emily's infancy we flew to the States—all three of us—in order to baptize her at the Freeville United Methodist Church. Like most things we did together during our brief time as a family, I was the tour guide and my husband the tourist, detached from the experience itself but ready with a camera to photograph it. He was a natural-born chronicler, used to looking at life through a lens, and of course because he was so often taking the picture, he was frequently missing from it. Our photo albums were mainly records of a mother and a daughter having experiences together, prefiguring our life to come.

My hometown church, next to the elementary school on Main Street, has always been one of my favorite places. Like everything else in Freeville, our church had become an exaggerated version of itself with the passage of time. In January, blanketed with snow, it looked like a New England white-steepled church such as you might see in a painting by Grandma Moses, but like much else in the village (including its inhabitants), up close it was obviously a little the worse for wear. It was faced with aluminum siding in the 1960s, and moisture in the joints between the metal clapboards forced little rust stains (they looked like rusty tears) down its front. A marquee with press-on letters announced that week's message—COME HOME TO JESUS.

Inside, the small narthex gave way to the warmth of the

sanctuary, which is wrapped in highly varnished maple wainscoting. Jesus stares benignly out at the congregation from his assigned place—high on the wall, next to the altar. Jesus' portrait, reproduced in the 1950s, has a muted, photo finish quality. It's a head-and-shoulders shot of Jesus, which in its pose and composition looks exactly like a high school yearbook picture. Jesus has a surfer smile, Tiffany blue eyes, a trim beard, and shoulder-length chestnut brown hair. He looks smart and nice. He's definitely the valedictorian of his class.

On Sundays when I was a kid, swinging my legs against the pew and hallucinating with boredom during the service, I'd stare at Jesus' yearbook picture and pray for him to deliver me from evil—and the agonies of the sermon. Whether due to divine intervention or good luck, I was spared both.

The United Methodist Church is not only a house of worship, but it is also the place where things happen in Freeville. The church is like a town hall, performance venue, and all-you-can-eat casserole buffet rolled into one. The congregation more or less runs itself according to an ambitious calendar made up not necessarily of holy days but of potluck suppers, coffee hours, barbecues, festivals, rummage sales, skits, cantatas, and hymn sings.

Many of our gatherings revolve around the eating of casseroles, pies, poultry, and any vegetable served in white sauce or Campbell's condensed cream of mushroom soup with shredded cheddar cheese and crumbled saltines on top. The church kitchen is staffed by a group of volunteer women who prepare and serve the meals by which we feed our faith. They engage in a cheddar cheese ministry of the highest order.

Among the kitchen ladies are my three aunts, Lena, Millie, and Jean. They wear aprons over their good clothes, their faces blurred by the steam rising from the massive pots they use to prepare their specialties—mashed potatoes, mashed squash, candied ham, or the church's legendary chicken barbecue.

On summertime Saturdays for the last fifty years a small committee of men have gathered at dawn at the barbecue pit across Main Street from the church. They lay out the coals and light them. By 8 A.M., the coals are white with heat, and they line up dozens of chicken halves on large wire racks, sopping them with a marinade-soaked brush. Within an hour the chickens start to cook and the vinegar scent of the marinade drifts through town.

When I was a kid I'd climb on my bike at the first whiff of barbecue and show up at the pit, hanging around and listening to the men talk about chickens, their jobs, their wives and kids, and what needed to be done to the old building to get it through another winter. I liked listening to these men talk. I never saw my own father at church—or the pit. These men were his age, but they weren't like him. They were gentle, witty, and tolerant, where my father was profane, sharp-edged, unpredictable, and opinionated. I was drawn to their devotion, expressed as it was through the delights of slow-cooking poultry.

The money raised would go back into the church, used to finance a new roof or for Sunday school materials, or put into a fund to send kids to Bible camp.

Church has also always been where my musical family sings together. My mother and aunts, cousins, sisters, and I are all natural-born harmonizers with perfect pitch who might have made something of ourselves, musically, except for the fact that along with all of our talent and natural show-offiness also came a stifling lack of ambition.

My sisters and I sang together in the youth choir, and a revolving chorus of my mother, aunts, and cousins sang in the adult choir. About twice a year—usually at Christmas and Easter—the church calendar brought all of us together in a case of harmonic convergence that sent shivers up my spine. Singing one of the grand old songs from the Methodist hymnal like "There Is a Balm in Gilead," I could hear my mother's, aunts', cousins', and sisters' voices blending in such a perfect braid of sound that it took me outside of myself.

It was the sound of my family's gene pool choir that first brought me into the mysterious community of faith and casseroles and made a believer out of me. Surely God had put my family together in such a place and dressed us in red flammable polyester robes in order to sing "The Angel Rolled the Stone Away" with one beautifully blended and pitched celestial Broadway voice underneath Jesus' year-book picture for a reason. He. She. Exists.

For her Freeville baptism, I dressed Emily—just three months old—in a long white Victorian christening gown that Rachel had given us, and our little family stood before my ample extended family (my mother, sisters, aunts, and cousins in their usual pews) and the rest of the small congregation while the minister brought her into the fold with a dab of holy water, a smear of oil, and a lit candle passed over her head. The congregation was asked to renounce the devil and then promised to be a witness to my child's spiritual life.

I looked out at the congregation from our place at the baptismal font and took solace in the fact that every last one of the people in the room had also faithfully borne witness to me. For better and worse, they abide.

After the baptism, we posed in the snow in front of the church together. The painted plywood nativity scene left over from Christmas was still up, and we briefly placed our baby on the straw of the empty manger and stepped back to enjoy the scene. I remember looking down at her and hoping that she would be blessed with moments of grace. I wondered if she would somehow bear the spiritual imprint of the community of faith and casseroles into which she had arrived.

As Emily grew I wanted her to understand and participate in the age-old rituals that had always given me so much comfort. Our lives, bifurcated as they were between city and country, were split spiritually too. In Washington we read from the poetic Book of Common Prayer and formally celebrated various feast days with special services and communion. The Episcopal service was beautiful, cerebral, and unchanging. The congregation was top-heavy with Washington luminaries—undersecretaries of state, Treasury Department officials, and other notables—including occasionally George and Barbara Bush and their Secret Service detail.

In Freeville, the service was hung onto the foundation of the Methodist lectionary, but it seemed to vary dramatically from week to week, based on what was happening around town. The most popular portion of the Methodist service was "Joys and Concerns," when any member of the congregation could stand up, speak his or her mind, and ask for prayers. Joys and Concerns would often gallop out of control, taking the worship service—and us—with it. The minister would dash up and down the aisle of the church like Phil Donahue, passing a microphone to congregants so they could have their say: "My mom's back went out again so now she's going to go to Syracuse for surgery."

"Donny's boss says they're doing another round of layoffs. We don't know what's going to happen yet."

"We're leaving the day after Christmas to go down to Florida to see our folks. We'd like travel prayers."

"Dad's pain is getting worse; they think it might be his kidneys this time."

"Oh, I don't need the microphone. I'll just yell. What I

wanted to say is that the JV team is doing really well this year, but the varsity lost again on Friday. The defense just can't get it together."

"I'm really happy to see Amy and Emily here again. I hardly recognized Emily, she's getting so tall! I hope we'll be seeing them in the choir while they're here."

Joys and Concerns is like the world's smallest radio station broadcasting the news of a very particular patch. Many of the headlines seem related to gallbladders, surgical procedures, and waiting on test results. Some of our news is sad and some is truly tragic, but the congregation also shares their triumphs—the new jobs, new grandchildren, or this year's bumper crop of zucchini. Joys and Concerns is where the community announces what is important. Then they ask for prayers and receive them. It is the most honest, fair, and just exchange I have ever witnessed.

STILL SMARTING FROM my Peanut Jesus debacle, Emily and I packed the car and drove north, where we rejoined the Freeville United Methodist Church broadcast. We left our big city church, with its staff of well-trained clergy, its historical significance, large endowment, massive charity efforts, and *Exorcist* movie tie-in and came home to a place that doesn't do communion very well but excels at community.

On Christmas Eve, Emily worked with the hardworking luminary committee, setting up the luminaries that run the entire length of Main Street. These were made of chopped-off plastic gallon milk jugs, weighted with sand and with a candle placed inside. In the daylight, these jugs, placed three feet apart and nestled into snowbanks, looked like the grubby remnants of recycle day. But in the dark, glowing from their candles, they lit a runway leading directly into the United Methodist Church. Our Christmas Eve service, crowded with families and fussy babies, ended, as it always did, with the lights dimmed as we sang "Silent Night" by candlelight. Everything got quiet.

We exited the church in silence, walking out onto Main Street. The luminaries were still flickering. Emily whispered, "Mom, check that out . . ."

Across the street, positioned under the pavilion of the barbecue pit, several members of the congregation had formed a living Nativity scene. The three Wise Men wore bathrobes knotted at the waist and dish towels on their heads. Mary's costume was a lovely royal blue; her hair was tied in a head scarf. She was gazing, lovingly, at a plastic doll positioned in the manger. Two painted plywood sheep grazed in the foreground.

Until that moment I had never quite understood the purpose of a living Nativity, where the object isn't to act out the Christmas story but to portray a fleshed-out but stationary tableau version of it. Looking at my neighbors dressed in their robes and dish towel headdresses I saw a life-size version of my cereal-box crèche.

"Mom, look—it's Mr. and Mrs. Eggleston. What are

they doing?" she whispered to me. I whispered in reply that they were going to stand there until midnight and that they were awaiting a Christmas miracle, just like all believers do on that night.

"Do you believe in miracles?" I asked Emily.

"Well, I did pray for something," she said.

I pictured her modest wish list for Santa Claus: it included ice skates, a sled, ski poles, and an elaborate American Girl doll play set, which I learned was out of stock when I had tried to order it—which was a good thing, because I couldn't afford it anyway.

"What did you pray for, honey?" I asked her. *Please let it be a Monopoly game, knitting needles and yarn—and the Polly Pocket veterinary clinic*, which I had purchased instead.

"I prayed for snow."

"Oh. Well, that's a nice thing to want on Christmas." I reflexively looked toward the sky and watched the steam from my breath float upward in a column of condensation. A cloud was passing in front of the moon, but otherwise the night was clear and struck with twinkling stars.

I looked at Sue and Keith Eggleston, now dressed up as Mary and Joseph. I had known them both since high school. They were standing as stock-still as the plywood sheep, trying to create a flesh-and-blood telling of an ancient story. A few cars driving down Main Street carrying last-minute shoppers home from Wal-Mart slowed to a crawl, their headlights sweeping across the scene.

I thought about what Reverend Kenworthy had said

about my ministry. Some people preach from the pulpit, moving people toward belief or action. Others, like our Freeville neighbors, minister by sharing their joys and concerns, by cooking and selling chickens, or by dressing in their bathrobes and standing in the cold while they demonstrate their faith to the community. All of us had something in common—the desire to show up, to be a witness to others, and to patiently await a miracle. I had introduced Emily to God. Eventually, she would see that when prayers go unanswered, you learn to change your prayers. She would learn that faith, like the seasons, comes and goes. I knew that I would return to Washington, go back into my classroom of little smart alecks, and try again.

Emily and I stood with our family in a small arc outside the barbecue pit, quietly watching the Nativity scene as the first flakes of snow started to drift down through the inky blackness of Christmas Eve.

SIX

Livestock in the Kitchen

The Many Uses of Cats

I CAN'T CLAIM to have a "way" with animals, though they do seem to have their way with me. When I look into the eyes of just about any animal—wild, farm raised, or domesticated—what I see staring back is a creature that will find a way to win me over—and then trample my spirit beneath its paw, flipper, or hoof.

My first grand devastation came in the form of a half ton of pure Holstein gristle. Her name was Shirley, and up to the day when we had to slaughter, butcher, and then eat her, she was a good cow. She was handsome and useful, and I, for one, loved her.

Shirley lived out the last decade of her life on our crumbling dairy farm with a herd of fifty fellow Holsteins who, like she, had more or less run out of options. If cows got what they deserved in life, then they'd preen and lounge in fields of clover, delicately balancing frosted cocktails between their hooves and smoking scented hookahs while discussing their most recent sexual encounters with Bill, the stud-muffin bull.

But life on our farm was not fair, and our small herd spent a goodly portion of their days huddled together in the barnyard, trying not to make eye contact with Bill the Bull, who glowered at them from his pen. Twice a day—at dawn and at dusk—they would stand shin deep in snow and mud, hanging patiently outside our broken-down barn, waiting for my father to bring them in and then relieve them of their milky burden.

Unlike the other cows, Shirley had been granted a human name, though my father didn't like to sentimental-ize and name the livestock. Mainly he referred to our cows as "The Girls," but sometimes he called them "Goddamn Filthy Bitches," especially when one of them shifted her weight and threatened to crush him, or when she forgot where her assigned stanchion was, or when she gave him a little kick as he was trying to clean her teats.

Like most farm kids I knew, I was ambivalent about the livestock. My siblings and I spent most of our time outside of school feeding them, shoveling up after them, and chasing them out of my mother's flower beds, where they headed every chance they got—because no amount of fencing could hold The Girls for long. Like Park Avenue debutantes, our Holsteins were high maintenance, moved in packs, and were immune to reasoning or punishment. Though we assumed that they were dumb as fence posts, they didn't have to outsmart us—they merely wore us down with repetition. Whatever they had done today, they would find a way to do again tomorrow.

The line between beasts of burden and beloved pets sometimes blurred in ways that caused discomfort, especially during the slaughtering season, when Shirley or the sweet calf I had taken care of and secretly named Miranda were shipped off to the slaughterhouse, destined to land back in our freezer as dinner. Looking back, I'm embarrassed to say that even in the face of these losses, I never so much as flirted with vegetarianism. In fact, such was the pragmatic food ethic in our household that when Shirley landed in our freezer, her meat was packed in brown butcher paper that was labeled with the date of her demise, along with her name.

11/06/72: Shirley.

Livestock were the source of our livelihood, and yet they were so much trouble (what with their constant eating, excretion, and escaping) that sometimes I would fantasize that if only our farm didn't have animals on it, then life would be just about perfect. I could definitely picture our family doing very well living on our hundred acres and enjoying an animal-free existence. There we are, gathered at the big dining room table, eating sharp cheese and pie and gazing out of gingham-curtained windows while my mother says, "More maple syrup, anyone?"

But farms—especially dairy farms—have a tendency to attract animals, and wherever livestock and humans intersect, life can get messy, bloody, brutish, violent, and sad.

With a series of unlucky parakeets at one end and the herd of put-upon bovines at the other, my family lived with, loved, despised, killed off, consumed, and cared about a fairly wide spectrum of the food chain. We were so surrounded by other species that we distinguished between "barn" and "house" animals. The cows, pigs, horse, chickens, geese, and one herd of scruffy cats stayed out. We also had cats, iguanas, a border collie, hamsters, turtles, and a formerly "baby" alligator that grew overly large living at one time or another inside the house. (Our house was also host to a gigantic colony of honeybees that established itself within the walls of my bedroom, coming and going as they needed, depending on the pollinating season.)

It wasn't until I was fully grown that I realized that sharing my childhood with animals had messed not only with portions of my childhood, but also with my tolerance for other, tidier ways of living. I was simply accustomed to dealing with food, fur, manure, and ornery animal-ness. Life without at least one other nonhuman species in it would always seem hollow, so I have found myself doomed to repeat this endless chaotic cycle of stewardship, love, and loss—and (of course!) I have been most drawn to that which I cannot control.

Unfortunately but perhaps not surprisingly—given our retrospective mismatch—my husband was allergic to nearly everything associated with life as I was used to living it. He wasn't merely allergic; he was allergic like a character in an antihistamine commercial. He was a projectile sneezer, a world-class wheezer, and a prodigious blooming rash and welt grower. A sniff of a buttercup, a bouquet of Queen Anne's lace, or even looking at a picture of goldenrod in a magazine could send his mucus flowing. Dander from dogs, cats, or horses brought on fits of explosively propellant sneezing.

I didn't notice this affliction so much when we first met as pet-less young college students, but as soon as we settled into life as a couple, living together in a tiny basement apartment in New York City, I started agitating for an animal—an apartment-friendly cat, specifically—and his allergies became a nonnegotiable medical issue. All the same, despite this chronic condition, I still tried to talk him into getting a pet.

We had just seen a commercial on television featuring cute-as-a-button kittens. One thing I always appreciated about my ex was his extreme susceptibility to cuteness. What I mean is that he had an abnormally elevated attraction to anything cute. Asian human babies and small animals of all kinds seemed especially to affect him.

The kittens on TV were tumbling over a big ball of

yarn. "God—look at them! Don't you think we should get a cat?" I implored. I'm not proud to say that I may have used a squeaky chew-toy voice that I employed from time to time—I was that desperate.

"Sorry. Allergic, remember?" he said, pointing to his nose.

"You know, they have shots for that. At first it's weekly, but after a few months they taper off," I offered.

"Ooh." He looked pained. "Don't you think that hurts the cat?" he asked.

I paused, one of those long pauses that you could probably drive a herd of cats through if you had a herd of cats, and I did not. I didn't even have one.

"Um, the shots are not for the *cat*. They're for the *human*," I said.

His shock was total, absolute, and very not cute. He simply could not imagine a person enduring something painful—on purpose. (But he evidently *could* imagine a shot that would render a cat hypoallergenic.)

I never brought it up again.

When my husband and I broke up, people who knew me well mentioned two things as being possible bright spots on my otherwise blighted life: weight loss and pet acquisition. I experienced both. I lost the requisite twenty pounds of worry weight and soon thereafter gained twenty pounds in tabby cat.

I met him right before Emily's birthday. Lord forgive me, I loved and claimed him at first sight, even though he wasn't technically "mine." He was given to Emily by her godmother, Martha, who knew me well enough to know that this particular dude, this young prince among pets, would be the answer to what ailed me.

"I've put him on hold so you can check him out before I give him to Emily," she told me, and so I raced down to a pet store in Georgetown and asked the clerk to retrieve him. The clerk came back a couple of minutes later holding an adolescent orange tiger cat. "He's pretty chill," the clerk told me and set him down on the counter next to the cash register, whereupon the extremely large kitten lay down and stretched out, draping a paw roughly the size of a hockey puck into the register's open cash drawer. I now realize that this was an omen. This particular cat would find a way to take my money.

"I think he's going to be sort of big-ish when he's filled out," the clerk said. I looked into the cat's calm and un-blinking orange eye. I thought of something my mother used to say to my sisters and me when our childhood squab-bles threatened to get out of hand: "Mark my words. This will end in tears."

He was delivered to our apartment in a super-size pet carrier—the kind most often used for Labrador retrievers. When the door to the carrier was opened, the cat sauntered out, looked around, and draped himself on the floor, as if he owned the place, which, of course, he would—in good time.

I've always preferred granting human names to animals,

so I was partial to calling our new cat Calvin Derrick, after one of my favorite ancestors. (I only knew Calvin Derrick through old-timey photographs, in which he was often surrounded by laughing women wearing stiff collars and straw hats.) Emily decided to name him Skunky, but thankfully the name didn't stick. Animals have a way of inhabiting or wiggling out of their given names. I've known a Skunky or two, and this cat was no Skunky.

It was October. Our cat was fat and orange, so Emily started calling him Pumpkin. He tried his name on for size and it fit.

Cats have a reputation for not being as interesting as dogs, but Pumpkin seemed to embody favored qualities of both species. He ran to the apartment door and greeted us with doglike enthusiasm when we came home, but he was lumpy and compliant enough to let Emily dress him in doll clothes—something few dogs with any self-esteem would tolerate. Pumpkin spent much of the first several months of his time with us dressed like "Felicity," a colonial-times doll that Emily owned. He wore a cape and bonnet willingly, though he didn't take to the lace-up boots. He participated in tea parties and safaris and treasure hunts. Sometimes we tied Emily's old baby blanket around his middle like a skirt, just because we could. He had a high tolerance for humiliation and a fondness for headgear, which is something of a prerequisite for being a member of our family.

At night, the cat split his time between our two rooms,

curling up with each of us in turn, placing his massive head on the pillow like a person.

As Pumpkin grew ever larger, topping out at twenty-two pounds, it became clear that his size would be one of his defining characteristics. When he was seated, his belly bulged over his haunches; from the back he had the silhouette of a snowman. Standing on his hind legs, which he could do surprisingly well, he was as tall as a kindergartner. Eating, eating, eating, and food were his main preoccupations, though he also loved to watch television and track the pigeons that would come to light on our windowsill.

One time my mother and I were talking on the phone about our cats—one of our favorite topics. We liked to trade anecdotes about them and then decide which movie stars would be best suited to playing them in a movie. One of Mom's cats, Blackie, a neurotic black-and-white foundling with tuxedo markings, was going through an anxiety-fueled upholstery-shredding phase. "He always looks like he's headed out to a sophisticated black-tie party with his tuxedo on," she said. "He's handsome, all right, like William Powell, but unfortunately he acts like Don Knotts." We decided that we would cast John Goodman to play Pumpkin in a movie, but only because Jackie Gleason was dead.

Every now and then I would catch a glimpse of Pumpkin's massive hindquarters and tail as he sauntered around the corner into the kitchen toward his bowl, and it would hit me: I am sharing my home with another species. I inhabit the same space as a four-legged thing covered in fur. I have livestock in my kitchen.

I didn't set out to complete our family by adding a pet to it—but that is what happened. This animal took the third chair, completing our family trio and bridging the gap of our loss. Emily and I projected onto him all of the qualities we most valued, and he went along with it. When we needed a playmate, we would drive him crazy by making him chase a feather or the light from our flashlight. When we needed a hug, we would hold him on his back and rub his belly like a dog, and he would fall asleep with his paws splayed in the air—paralyzed. When Emily had kids over to play, they would take the cat into her room and spend hours following him, talking to him, and trying to carry him around. We decided that he was hilarious. When we had been out and he was alerted to our return by the sound of the key in the door, we could hear his heavy footfall as he bounded across the apartment toward the door, as if to say, "Where were you? I've been worried sick!"

To make our frequent trips to Freeville, we would shove Pumpkin into his carrier for the seven-hour-long drive. He grew so used to the routine that eventually we could leave the carrier's door open and know that he would essentially just hang out. In Freeville, Pumpkin led the life of a country cat; we let him go outdoors, and he would stalk the backyard, occasionally catching a rodent by accident and then acting horrified by what he had done. He staked out a spot on the bank of Fall Creek, and I could look out of the kitchen window and see the outline of his massive silhouette as he sat and tried to watch the water while swallows from my neighbor's barn dive-bombed him in an unrelenting course of harassment.

At night, when the village was silent, Pumpkin would travel across Main Street to visit with the neighborhood cats. Our neighbors directly across the street, the Joneses, had a series of muscular bruisers over the years that were all named Indiana. (Unlike our family, the Joneses liked to stick with one cat name, regardless of the cat, though all of the many "Indiana Joneses" I have known over the years do seem to share a certain swashbuckling quality.) Though Emily and I imagined that Pumpkin was happily playing poker and smoking cigars with Indiana Jones and his crew of local feline hoodlums in a cat version of *Guys and Dolls*, we heard nighttime howling and knew that he was getting into scrapes. Like us, Pumpkin was a part-time resident, and certain lifestyle adjustments needed to be made. "You can't just show up from the big city and expect everyone to accept you right away," we'd tell him as we dressed his bloody ear. "Back off a little. Be a listener. Don't go on too much about how great you have it in the city. These cats catch their own food and have never met a sardine straight from the can."

Unfortunately, like our long-ago Holsteins, Pumpkin was a slow learner—or a masochist. I heard from neighbors that he would roam their backyards at night, yowling under the occasional window, looking for trouble but evidently too slow to outrun it when it happened. I used to marvel that this cat, accustomed to nine hundred square feet of apartment living, could come to the country, ramble so far away at night, and then still find his way home. Some nights I would lie awake worrying about him, imagining him getting hurt or lost. I couldn't figure out how he would know where we lived and wondered if maybe he'd find a better deal elsewhere and just not bother coming back to us. Our neighbor Penny had five handsome cats, some of them hungry refugees originally from the Section 8 housing one block away on Railroad Street. When Penny took in a cat, he or she got a literary name plucked from George Eliot or Dickens, a leather collar, two square meals a day, free and excellent health care, and the freedom to lounge on her Stickley furniture and watch movies. Penny's house must have seemed like Club Med to these Section 8 kitties. What cat wouldn't want that? I'd move in with her if she'd take me.

Rachel's new husband, my brother-in-law Tim, helped me to understand an animal's instinct and desire to come home. Tim is a bird expert who works at Cornell University's Lab of Ornithology and is a well-known falconer who flies birds all over the world. Tim raises birds of prey as well as a flock of homing pigeons at his house down the street from ours in Freeville. One evening I was standing in back of Rachel and Tim's house, watching the sky as it turned from dusk to dark. Suddenly, his flock of birds came wheeling across the sky—thirty birds flying in concert. They made a grand loop over the playground at the elementary school and then dropped their speed and altitude and, one by one, flew into the large coop that Tim keeps in the backyard. These birds leave in the morning, cover a huge territory each day, and return at dusk to a coop behind a house on Main Street. I couldn't get over it. "How do they know where to go and why do they always come back?" I asked Tim. "Well, they come back here because this is where they live. This is their home," he told me. "Oh yeah," I said. "I do that too, come to think of it."

And so our cat always came back too, because his home was with us.

I should have expected that Pumpkin's prodigious appetite would get him into a serious jam one day, but unfortunately I didn't quite see the role I played in his lifestyle choices. I was like the bewildered mother who goes on *Dr. Phil* wondering why her 850-pound bed-bound son is so fat. Our cat had no "off switch" on his appetite, and I never denied him anything. Though I always considered myself a responsible parent to Emily, unfortunately I didn't apply the same standards to my stewardship of our most vulnerable, obese, and charming family member. Belying the stereotype of the cat as a finicky, careful eater, ours was a Hoover in a cat suit with no culinary standards.

One Christmas season I was so broke that I decided to make—rather than buy—all of that year's Christmas gifts. I have done this poverty-inspired "homemade Christmas" any number of times, and it has never worked out for me or for any of my recipients, as far as I can tell. I am crafty to a fault, by which I mean that anything handmade by me is usually delivered along with the phrase "I'm sorry. It's all my fault."

This particular year, my friend Margaret talked me into making biscotti to give as gifts. Biscotti are Italian cookies, baked twice and at low temperature until they are hard enough to be used as a building material. Margaret thought it would be a good choice for me. Because of its natural bricklike consistency, nobody could ever wonder if the cookie was stale. Margaret shared her favorite recipe and talked me through the steps. I successfully turned out a couple of batches of almond cookies—just enough to distribute to family members who had never heard of the exotic baked good and who would most likely toss them directly onto the compost pile on Christmas night as a treat for the woodchucks.

My gift was finished, packaged in tins I'd gotten from the Dollar Store, and sitting on the kitchen counter for a few days until the weekend, when we would drive to Freeville for the holiday.

Pumpkin wasn't himself. I knew this because he had stopped eating. A day or two of this wouldn't really hurt, I figured, but then he stopped drinking. He grew even more lethargic than usual, and his orange eyes seemed to lose their shine. His bulk started to disappear at an alarming rate.

By the time I got him to the twenty-four-hour emergency vet, it was December 23 and he was floppy and not breathing well. They x-rayed him and discovered that he had eaten an almond that had most likely fallen onto the kitchen floor during my baking binge; the nut was stuck crosswise in his gut. Pumpkin would need surgery right away to remove it. The vet thought that if they hydrated the cat for several hours on an IV he would probably be able to make the long drive from DC to Freeville. Emily and I picked him up at 2 A.M. and raced him to the School of Veterinary Medicine at Cornell (ten miles from our house on Main Street) in an ice storm, our lightweight Saturn sedan fishtailing on the black ice. The vet in DC called ahead, and when we arrived at around noon on Christmas Eve, white-coated interns met us in the parking lot to run him into surgery.

I called my sister Anne from the hospital. Unlike me, Anne really does have a way with animals. She's had a variety of adventures involving three-legged dogs, blind cats, and goats, and had even toyed with raising alpacas (or was it llamas?) at one time. She is famous in our family for being able to stuff a pill down the gullet of any animal and then covering its nostrils so that it won't spit the pill back up. Anne also seemed to absorb the most pragmatic lessons from the animals of our childhood. "If he goes into surgery, it's going to be expensive. You need to think about whether you want to do that. If he's suffering now and then has surgery, he might not come through it and it's still going to cost you. You just need to think about it," she said.

Our childhood had taught us too much about how animals die. As our various beloved pets neared the ends of their lives—if they were lucky enough not to die unexpectedly under a car or in a tractor tire, freeze to death in the snow, or as happened with one cat, expire in the clothes dryer with a load of clothes—our father was frank about what needed to be done. When I was around ten years old and our very dear twenty-three-year-old calico house cat, Mickey, was too sick and feeble to function, he gathered his children together and explained the options. "I could put her into the truck and take her up to the vet and have him do it," he said. "But you know how much she hates to ride in the truck and I don't know if it's right for her to be so scared at the end." We nodded our heads. Mickey would have been frantic during the ride; I couldn't stand the thought of it. Dad said, "Or I can do it here." We said that he could.

My father raised animals for a living, and it went against his nature to kill things. I knew that about him. I also knew that he started each day stroking a cat curled on his lap as he drank his first cup of coffee at the kitchen table. He was a tough guy who also happened to be an unreconstructed cat man. He got his gun. We stayed inside the house, quiet, until it was done. In time, he came back into the house. I was crying; I already missed Mickey, who used to sit on my lap and drink milk out of my spoon as I ate my cereal in the morning.

"She was sitting in the sun. She never even felt it. I buried her over there," he said, gesturing toward the edge of the yard. And though I know that it sounds like a cruel thing to do, I knew that he had done a very hard thing, and that it had been a kindness. I never doubted it—then or now. Anne and I shared this history, and though we didn't bring it up, we both knew that when you love an animal, you have to love it, literally, to death.

The vet tried to explain to me what was going on. I was told that surgery might not save our cat and that if it did he would be facing a long recovery in the hospital. I heard myself say, "Do whatever you need to do. Please do it." I signed some papers and they took the cat away. I was prompted to stop at the cashier's office on my way out, where I wrote a check for a $100 deposit that I didn't have the funds to cover.

On Christmas day, everyone in my family pretended to marvel over their biscotti and asked about the cat. They talked about him the way you discuss a missing family member at a reunion—very fondly and optimistically. "You know what I like about him? He's a gentleman," my mother said. I pictured Pumpkin wearing a waistcoat and monocle. Emily and I drove over to the hospital in the afternoon to check on him. Cornell's animal hospital is very large and fancy, as befits a huge university research facility. As we waited to see the vet on call, a few other Christmas visitors came through, stomping the snow off their boots onto the waiting room floor. "I'm here to see Muffin," "I'm visiting Peaches," "I brought a deer in the other day and I'm just checking in to see how it's doing?"

Pumpkin was brought out to us on a gurney. He was

heavily bandaged and on an IV. He looked up at us—the light back in his eyes—and then gave one switch of his tail, as if to say, "I'm baaaaaack." We petted him and cooed over him and then, elated, drove home to Freeville to tell the family. We visited him twice a day during the week he was in the hospital. When he was ready to come home I couldn't get to the hospital fast enough. Before they would bring him out to me, however, I was led, once again, to the dreaded cashier. The bill, thoughtfully itemized, was $1,500. I excused myself and called my sister again from the hallway.

"They want fifteen hundred dollars! I don't know what to do!" I whispered. I pictured myself working off the bill by giving enemas over at the large animal clinic. My sister sighed. "You have to realize something. They really don't want to keep your cat. Their goal is to give him back to you today. So they'll take whatever they can get from you now. Negotiate a payment plan for the rest," she said. I couldn't imagine anyone not wanting to keep our cat, but glancing out over the waiting room (one Newfoundland with a bandaged leg, three kittens, a pair of frisky terrier twins, and a snake), I had to concede that, for these people, Pumpkin was very much beside the point.

Our cat limped back into our lives; he had lost half of his body weight, and we babied him and fed him special prescription cat food ($58/case) until he bulked up again.

I read a story in the paper recently claiming that, according to archaeologists, cats domesticated themselves. Humans originally domesticated and bred dogs to do jobs and be companions. But thousands of years ago, cats started choosing to be around humans, because when people began to cultivate grain, the grain stores were host to rodents that cats fed upon. Cats were first motivated to be around humans because we were a food source for them. Staying with humans was very much their choice.

Pumpkin took this evolutionary notion a step further. He domesticated us. He bent us to his will in his benevolent, furry way. He put a subject in our sentences. When Emily was away from home visiting her father or at camp, I would send her letters outlining the cat's activities and grievances, his many complaints about being in my sole care, and his threats to hire a lawyer, should she not return forthwith. I would tell her on the phone that I was fine and keeping busy, but that Pumpkin was a little lonely and couldn't wait to see her again. Indeed, when she was away, he would wander into her room, cocking his giant head, looking for her. When we took long trips, we'd occasionally bring him with us and sneak him into hotel rooms, concealed beneath a garbage bag and sweaters. He would eat his Friskies out of an ashtray in the bathroom. During breakfast at our apartment, Emily would let him sit on top of the kitchen table and drink her sweet milky leftovers, the way Mickey used to.

Pumpkin waddled toward the end of his life slowly and sweetly. He became particular, like the old man at a church supper who can't decide what to put on his plate. He grew svelte, thin even, and one day I saw him wobble and lose his balance. It was summer, and we were in our little house on Main Street. Pumpkin was spending much of his time stretched out on the cool floor of the porch.

Our vet, Gry, is also a neighbor. She was born in Denmark, but now she and her family live on a small, tidy farm at the edge of the village limits. Her husband is a farrier who raises and works a team of huge and handsome horses. One summer evening I was driving up the road past their place as the sun's last rays were glancing across the field near their house. Gry's husband was in the field, standing on a thresher being pulled by a team of horses, mowing the field in the ancient way.

Gry felt a mass in Pumpkin's abdomen that for once wasn't his lunch, and she ordered an ultrasound. Emily held and stroked him as he lay on his side, purring, while the technician worked. The news was terrible. He had lymphoma. Like an experienced therapist working with a depressed client, Gry automatically held out a tissue box as she told us. I took one tissue and then another and then I decided to cut out the middleman and asked her to give me the box.

She said that Pumpkin could have surgery, but that even with the surgery, she didn't expect him to last the summer. "Either way, I'm sorry to say that Pumpkin won't be going back with you this fall," she said. She pursed her lips. She had gotten to know him over the years. She looked at him, stretched out on the examination table. "Oh yes. What a good boy he is," she said. We agreed that he was a fine cat.

We decided against the surgery, but this time, it wasn't about the money. We had to try to answer the question that people who love animals have to make on their behalf: How will this end? The last weeks of his life, Pumpkin spent his time slowly prowling the place, marking his extensive territory throughout Freeville with his presence for the last time. We hung out together, and as I worked in my little upstairs office overlooking the creek, he'd check in on me and lie at my feet. Then he'd wait at the top of the stairs for me to carry him down.

The day Pumpkin was euthanized it was beastly hot and the air was still. Emily's godfather, Kirk, my oldest friend from childhood, was visiting us from Maine with his wife, Camille, and their teenage daughters, Hannah and Alice. Kirk said that he would help to dig a hole to bury Pumpkin in the backyard, and I took a box and a towel along with me to bring his body home from the vet's.

At Gry's clinic, she has a separate room with a separate entrance for the animals that are going to be killed, presumably so that those who are carrying dying or dead animals don't have to pass through the more public waiting room on their way to and from the car. The room is serene and pretty. There are curtains on the windows and framed poems and quotes on the wall with passages from Walt Whitman, Shakespeare, and the Bible. I sat in a rocking chair with the cat in my lap and told him one last time that I treasured his eleven years with us. I said that I would never forget him, just as I've never forgotten any of the livestock that have graced my life, even while they have occasionally trampled it.

By the time I got home it was ninety-nine degrees. The air was heavy, and the trees limp. Kirk and his family had gone to pick up Emily, who was working as a counselor at a local camp. The house was empty, but even allowing for the absence of the cat, something seemed different. I looked around. Before they left, Kirk and Camille had gathered Pumpkin's food bowls, washed them out, cleaned out his litter boxes, and cleaned up some spots in the house where he had been sick. I couldn't believe that they had thought to do that. Kirk doesn't even like cats, though he always claimed that Pumpkin, by virtue of his attractiveness, personality, and presence in our family, was a special case.

When Kirk and his family returned home with Emily, I was sitting in an Adirondack chair in the backyard; I had finished crying and was drinking a beer. They formed an arc around me, looking down at me with concern. For the first time in a couple of weeks, I turned my full attention toward the people in my life. What magnificent creatures they are! I first met Kirk in fourth grade, and we've been close friends ever since. He had embraced his role as a special person in Emily's life and was in touch frequently. He was always available to step in and do "guy things" if we needed. He knew that he had an opportunity to be a positive influence in Emily's life and he took it seriously, traveling from Maine to attend birthdays or school events and always sending postcards and gifts from his other travels. Our families had become extremely close, trading visits each summer, and whenever they came to Freeville, Kirk baked Emily's favorite blueberry pie and also grabbed a paintbrush and managed to do some home maintenance for us.

Emily looked down at me. Her long chestnut brown hair was shiny in the sun. The heat formed a milky halo around her. "Mom, are you OK?" I raised my hand and shielded my eyes with the Heineken bottle. It was cool and sweaty against my cheek. "I'm OK, honey. And you?" "Me too," she said.

I told them that because of the heat, I had decided to have Pumpkin's body cremated, and that was partly true, but mostly I couldn't bear the thought of handling his dead body. We picked a spot on the bank of the creek where we would bury his ashes when we received them. A few days later, I got a call from Gry to pick up his ashes. Pumpkin came back to us in a round metal tin from the Dollar Store—*exactly* like the tins I had packaged my ill-fated biscotti in so many years ago. We kept the tin on our kitchen counter for several weeks, and then the evening before we drove back to the city for the start of school, Emily and I went out to the creek, dug a deep hole, and set it in.

SEVEN

Failing Up

I DIDN'T BECOME an advice columnist on purpose. It's not the sort of job a person can train for, after all. Like much of my work life, this latest opportunity seemed a case of failing up. Failing up is a specialty of mine. It happens at low points when a certain sort of plucky confidence meets with luck in the form of unexpected circumstances. It happens when you kick yourself for not picking up that dime you saw on the sidewalk, only to find a dollar on the next block.

I've always felt like the lazy leftover in my family of worker bees. Like a caterpillar at a picnic, I feel most comfortable grazing around the edges, inch-worming my way in and out of situations. I've worked at a bicycle repair shop, I've cleaned hotel rooms and been a receptionist. I've held jobs that other people didn't want, but I've never taken a job *I* didn't want. The way I see it, in a pinch I can always work the overnight shift at a 7-Eleven—to use an example of a job I definitely don't want. I'm fairly sure that I wouldn't be a very good convenience store clerk, partly because I'd drink my wages in Slushies; however, probably because I grew up on a farm, any work that doesn't involve shoveling manure ultimately seems pretty cushy. Manure is like that—it has a way of affecting a person's standards. As it turned out, working with manure as a child prepared me nicely for making television, which was my first in a series of careers.

Years ago, when I lived in New York with my husband and worked as a television producer, I used to ride the city buses to and from the office. During the ride, out of idleness and in order to avoid contact with my fellow commuters, I'd stare at the little posters over the bus's windows advertising job training for various careers. Though I liked my job, I was under no illusions about it. Making television is hardly a high calling. The hour-long show I worked for specialized in the sort of low-rent exploitive story that is commonplace now but seemed new, if not particularly fresh, when we were doing it. We excelled at "Tragedy in the Heartland" stories, which we balanced out with "How the Mighty Have Fallen" pieces. For a time, during the mid-1980s, I did little else but stand with my camera crew on crowded sidewalks outside Manhattan courthouses covering the "perp walks" of Wall Street tycoons brought down by insider trading scandals. "Tycoon in the Slammer" stories were especially popular around the holidays.

My commute down Manhattan's West Side more or less ruined me for long-term job satisfaction working in television because the ads lining the bus filled my head with dreams of making a living doing something I considered useful.

On my arrival home, I'd say to my husband, "Welding seems like a very lucrative and rewarding career."

"You said that yesterday about law enforcement," he'd remind me.

My husband knew I had a soft spot for law enforcement, where I was certain that some of my more surprising qualities—physical strength on a small frame, the ability to yell loudly, and an uncanny knack for hiding in plain sight—would serve me well. "They don't let just anybody join the FBI academy. You have to be physically and mentally agile to withstand eighteen months of grueling training in Quantico, Virginia," I'd mumble, but he'd heard it all before.

For me, the two hardest questions to answer have always been: Who am I? and What do I want? In my early professional life, I dipped in and out of jobs drifting toward an answer until I finally arrived at the one career that truly seemed to be my calling. Once I had Emily I finally knew what I wanted to do with my life. Being a mother completed my résumé. I shocked everyone who knew me—and even surprised myself a little—by wanting to stay home and be a full-time wife and mother. My husband liked this plan. He told me, "I just want you to be happy!" and I believed him until he left me with the baby and moved to Russia with his girlfriend.

Divorce clarified so much for me. Without any backup parenting, I stopped worrying about having a career. I chose to work at jobs that served my family. After moving to Washington, I found a niche doing work that served other people's families too—as a freelancer filling in for women on maternity leave. My first office jobs after my divorce were as a receptionist and a booker (filling in for a long-term employee having twins), securing guests for shows on National Public Radio. At 5:30 P.M., just as *All Things Considered* was winding down, I'd race out of the building and over to Emily's school to pick her up from her after-school program. If I hit a traffic snag or other delay, I'd feel like my head would explode. No deadline in the news business ever prepared me for the pressure of after-care pickup. Emily's school had a zero-tolerance policy for lateness. Parents were charged $20 for each five minutes after 6 P.M., and worse than that, the late children were brought out to the curbside like tomorrow's recycling, where they stood with a caregiver until the parent arrived. Sometimes I was the last mother to arrive for pickup, and I'd find Emily waiting with her backpack on over her coat. One time I asked her,

"Does it make you nervous when I'm last? Do you worry that I'll forget to come get you?"

"No, I don't worry about that. I mean, you always *do* come, so I think you always *will* come," she said. Her faith in me far exceeded my faith in myself. There were nights after work when I was too tired for dinner. We'd get dinner at the drive-through Burger King, limp home, take a bath, and be in bed by eight. More than once I sent her to school with an empty lunch box because in my rush to get out of the house in the morning, I'd forgotten to fill it.

I kept begging the producer of *All Things Considered* to let me do radio stories, and she finally told me to stop asking and just do it, and so I did. She found a part-time desk job for me during school hours (filling in for someone having a difficult pregnancy with mandated bed rest), and I worked producing commentaries and writing my own. When I needed to, I would bring Emily into the office and studio, happy that she was being exposed to creative people who worked in such an interesting medium. In between stints at NPR, I worked as a substitute teacher at Little Folks School, Emily's former nursery school (a spate of pregnancies among the staff meant plenty of work for me). Trying to corral the class's toddlers into "circle time" reminded me of various former bosses of mine in television; I instinctively knew how to handle them.

When Emily was in sixth grade, I got a call from *Time* magazine's new Washington bureau chief. He said he had been hearing me on the radio and wanted to talk to me about a job at the magazine. We met and he offered me a staff position as a writer. Reluctantly, I said no. I couldn't imagine taking on a job that would require sixty-hour work weeks and travel. He said, "Forgive me for asking, but not a lot of people turn down these jobs. Do you mind telling me why?"

"I have another job," I said.

"I didn't realize that. Could you tell me what it is?" he asked.

"I'm trying to raise a person," I told him. The elevator arrived with cinematic timing, and I got on it. If this were a movie, my future boss would have stopped the closing door with his hand in order to offer me something more acceptable, but this wasn't a movie and I took the Metro home from my meeting, kicking myself.

I had thought that asserting my needs and values in this way would feel good, but it didn't. I went home to my kid, feeling like a loser. Actually, I felt worse than a loser. I felt like a freelancer. My professional future as a maternity fill-in niche worker was tied up with other women's birth choices. Frankly, ovulation—even my own—had always made me sort of nervous; now I realized that I had become a job doula. *Right now, a midlevel female journalist is having sex; in eight and a half months I'll have her job*, I thought. It gave me that not-so-fresh feeling.

The defining characteristic of failing up is that the turning point happens at the lowest point of the failure cycle, and so it happened here. Several days after I turned down the job at *Time*, the bureau chief called me back, praised my family values, and offered me a job writing a column about families and parenting. I would be in the office two days a week and then work from home. I would be well paid in a job that wasn't tied to another woman's family planning and maternity choices. This was a position with absolutely no connection to fallopian tubes. I took it.

"You know that you skipped over the part where you work here for years and then get your own column?" he said.

"Yeah, I know. I skipped over that part," I said.

The last couple of years of the twentieth century were good for me, professionally. I wrote my column and had a nice office downtown, complete with smart colleagues who would occasionally have lunch with me. Emily and I moved into a larger apartment in our same building where we each had our own bathroom. I started paying my bills in the same month they were due. At night we would sit in our front room, looking out onto the twinkling lights of Connecticut Avenue. My work was flexible enough that I could write the column from Freeville during the summer; I set up an office in the back bedroom, overlooking Fall Creek.

September 11, 2001, changed everything for a lot of people, and it changed everything for us. I could see the smoke over the Pentagon from my downtown office. My boss asked me to cover a press conference outside the Capitol building where representatives of the legislative branch of our government stood on the sidewalk, looking like a tour group that had lost its way. (The rest of Congress had been spirited to a mountain vault in West Virginia.) A lone camera crew had set up a tripod on the lawn of the Capitol; the crew trained their camera toward the Capitol building and then sat in lawn chairs on the grass facing away from the building, waiting for the apocalypse.

As soon as I could, I jumped onto the Metro and raced to Emily's school. The train was crowded with stunned government workers escaping downtown. Their government ID badges jangled against their chests as the train swayed back and forth. No one spoke. At school, the seventh graders were gathered together in the gym. The girls were group hugging; the boys milled around looking confused. I walked Emily home. Connecticut Avenue was crowded with well-dressed professional refugees too scared to take public transportation—all of us furtively scanning the sky for more signs of attack. "If anything else happens and we get separated, I want you to head north," I told her. My daughter had just started riding the bus by herself, but somehow I saw Emily making her way three hundred miles due north to Freeville. I knew my mother would give her pancakes for dinner. "And north is . . . ?" Emily asked. "That way," I said, pointing up the avenue.

By September 12, I was out of a job. *Time* magazine had found a new focus, and there was no more room in the magazine for the sort of "How to get your baby to sleep through the night" stories that were my specialty.

With no job and no job prospects, this left plenty of time for me to fretfully plan escape routes from the city in the event of an emergency. All through that terrible fall, as the anthrax scare hobbled our mail service and a dusting of confectioners' sugar fallen off a doughnut could cause a citywide panic, I would lie awake at night reviewing the map of Washington in my head and plotting the fastest and safest way out. The route varied, but my mental compass always pointed north toward home. I was grateful to be from a place so inconsequential that no one would think to attack it.

I used to wonder why old people are always glued to the Weather Channel. Now I know it's because watching a weather system form over the Great Plains gives them a three-day focus for their anxiety ("Velma—there's a low-pressure system over Nebraska; get out the candles!"). After the September 11 attacks, jobs in Washington dried up. I couldn't even find a pregnant woman to fill in for, so I started living off credit cards. I also became our family's safety officer. I attended a seminar at a local college at which we were urged to stock up on duct tape and plastic in case we had to seal ourselves into our home in the eventuality of a chemical attack. We were told to have a three-day supply of food and water on hand.

I went directly from the seminar to a supermarket and hurriedly browsed the aisles for our emergency supply. Unfortunately, I've always thought that granola bars taste like plywood and I'm not much of a water drinker, though I do enjoy just about every other beverage. I thought about it. If we were trapped in our apartment, would we want to eat raw soy while we waited, probably pointlessly, for help to arrive? I filled my basket with Twizzlers, Mister Salty pretzels and Diet Coke—my PMS diet. I also picked up an extra bag of Friskies for the cat. It was quite obvious to me that Pumpkin was one of those frightening apartment cats you see in the tabloids who eat their owners under duress. Lately I thought I'd seen a certain look in his orange eyes; in the event of a terrorist attack, I wanted him to remain well fed.

I packed our stash, along with a flashlight and some extra batteries, in an old suitcase and put it near the door. Emily asked me for a Diet Coke. "You could have it now and regret your choice later when we're in our hazmat suits and there's nothing to drink, but honestly it's up to you," I sniffed, though we did agree to split one pack of Twizzlers before dinner.

I was seriously contemplating cutting our losses in Washington and moving back to Freeville (where I knew I could get a job at Clark's Sure Fine Food Mart) when I read in the paper that Ann Landers had died in Chicago. Unbeknownst to me, the legendary advice columnist's passing was my own personal weather system forming over the Great Plains. Eventually the storm would gain strength, move east, suck us up into its funnel cloud, and carry us back to the Midwest.

Jim Warren, a friend and editor at the *Chicago Tribune*, had tossed some freelancing assignments my way during my leanest times. When Ann Landers died, I sent Jim an e-mail saying, "Now *that's* a job I'd take. Ha Ha Ha Ha." Jim told me that the *Tribune* had no plans to replace Ann Landers, and I assured him I was joking. Ha Ha Ha. About a month after this exchange, Jim contacted me and said the paper was going to try to launch a new column; he invited me to try out.

It was summertime, and Emily and I were staying in our little house in Freeville. Jim e-mailed me five pretty typical advice questions and told me to take a week to answer them. I checked them out. One was about two cousins who had had a brief affair; one was about a family of siblings fighting over their father's possessions while their father lay dying; one was a fairly standard question about wedding etiquette. Jim said the newspaper had several candidates and that we had all been given the same questions and the same week-long deadline. I decided to tackle the work right away because, frankly, I didn't have much else to do.

Like many jobs I've gone after, I had a fairly neutral attitude about this one at the outset. I thought there was a chance I could fail my way up into it, but the prospects seemed even slimmer than usual. It wasn't until I started doing it that I realized how much I wanted to be an advice columnist for a living. After all, a good advice columnist is at least as useful as a welder or an FBI agent.

It was a hot afternoon. My hometown had settled into its daily midafternoon doldrums. As I read and then contemplated the problems of these complete strangers, I realized that I was in the perfect position to offer advice to people. It's not that I'm a natural at giving advice—in fact, I couldn't think that I'd ever been asked my opinion on a personal dilemma—but as the plankton at the end of my family's food chain, I have been on the receiving end of plenty of advice (all of it unsolicited). I thought of my mother and her three older sisters and of my own two older sisters. In my family, the advice flows downward, and I'm at the bottom of the hill holding a bucket.

I e-mailed my audition column back to Jim that afternoon. He replied, "You have a week so please take it. I'm not even going to look at this." I thought about it. I knew I could jump on my bike, ride down to my mother's house, and run everything past her. I could get my aunts and older sisters to weigh in. But then I realized that I had already absorbed and appropriated the voices of the women in my life. I already knew what I was supposed to know. I decided to wing it on my own. "Go ahead and read it. This is my final answer," I replied.

The *Tribune* took all of the audition columns and test-marketed them for groups of newspaper readers. In every single test market, the result was the same: readers' first choice for an advice columnist was to bring Ann Landers back from the dead.

Once bringing Ann Landers back from the dead was ruled out as a possibility, it was decided that I would do.

On my first trip to Chicago, I got out of the cab in front of the *Tribune*'s magnificent Gothic building on Michigan

Avenue, twirled around in the street, and threw my hat into the air like Mary Tyler Moore. I didn't actually do that, of course. I got out of the cab and my hat fell off of my lap onto the street and the cab ran over it on its way to pick up another passenger, but my prospective employers offered me the job anyway.

Now I had to break the news to the kid.

I was driving with Emily along a particularly pictur-esque stretch of a parkway in Washington when I decided to give her full access to my awesomeness. I had read an article that kids and parents often have meaningful conver-sations in the car. Emily and I had of course already had plenty of meaningful conversations—sometimes in the car and sometimes shouted tearfully through the closed bath-room door—but I admit to deliberately setting the stage for this talk, because this conversation was going to be mem-orable as well as meaningful. It turned out to be both.

"Well, I have great news. I got the job!" I'm not sure why, but I seemed to be shouting.

"Mom—that's great! Yay! I'm so happy for you!" she shouted back.

"So we're going to move to Chicago like we talked about," I exclaimed. I was a puppy pawing the air for atten-tion.

"Yeah—that's right, I remember," she said.

I was wondering if it would be possible to both steer the car forward and physically reach back with my right hand in order to pat myself on the back. Would the seat belt have enough play for me to lean forward and reach between my own shoulder blades? I hoped so.

We were quiet for a second.

Emily said, "I'll be able to finish school here, right?" (She was currently in the eighth grade.)

I thought about it. It was February and I was starting the job in July. "Of course you can finish school here. No problem!" I said.

We rode along, each enveloped in her own thoughts. I was mentally packing our apartment, a fantasy process that involved pitching garbage bags filled with our lesser possessions out the window and onto Connecticut Avenue, eight stories below. After fantasy packing, I moved on to dreaming of a paycheck. I hadn't had one of those in a long, long time. It was one whole presidential administration ago since I'd had a job of any consequence. I was distressed to realize that my luck seemed to run out on roughly the same timetable as Bill Clinton's.

Emily and I rode along quietly for a few moments before I got that familiar sinking sensation. It was a slow dawning of the sort a cartoon character reveals just before the grand piano drops on her head.

I looked sidelong at my daughter. "When you say you want to finish school, you mean . . . ?"

"My senior year," she said.

Emily was clear on this issue. She would be happy to move to Chicago—in four years.

I pulled the car over. We were in a leafy neighborhood in a town I had always loved and which we would now be leaving. I had made some bonehead choices in my checkered work life, but I had never before packed up and moved for a job. In my mind, moving is what you did for people, not for work.

I realized that in the several months I had been trying out for and wrangling over this job, I hadn't ever given Emily the unvarnished truth about it. In our life together, I always maintained the fiction that we were in complete control of our destinies, so I had never prepared Emily for the eventuality of a grand piano falling from the sky. I turned toward my girl. "We're going. I'm sorry; I know it's hard, but we are."

Emily is the most even-tempered person I've ever known, but those rare times when she is angry are fearsome. I saw the irises of her eyes go from chestnut to black. Cyclones and tornadoes raced across her pupils. I wondered if she could set me on fire with only the power of her adolescent mind. I was quite sure that she wanted to.

Watery tears chased the storms away, and we rode home in silence.

The swearing commenced soon after. True to her nature, Emily picked her moment well. She waited until the next morning when we were getting ready for church. I awoke to that morning's Sunday *New York Times*, which carried a half-page story with a headline reading "Possible

Successor to Ann Landers Named" accompanied by a small headshot of me alongside a large full-length photo of Ann Landers. Perhaps the photo placement wasn't deliberate, but I looked like a pipsqueak next to the late legend, who was shown standing jauntily in her palatial Chicago apartment. The article implied that I was plucked from obscurity to take the advice column job, and though that makes a nice story, it isn't quite true—I wasn't really that obscure, certainly in my own mind.

Emily stood behind her closed bedroom door—the one she knew I could hear through, especially if I pressed my ear against it, which I of course did. I listened in horror as my daughter quickly ran down George Carlin's checklist of the seven most unspeakable words and then added whole categories of epithets of her own invention. Listening in, I played my own little mental *Jeopardy!* game of foul-mouthed invective.

"Alex? I'll take 'Where My Mother Can Shove It' for $500."

"What is: 'Where the sun don't shine'?"

"Let me try 'The Lord's Name in Vain for $1,000.'"

It went on like this for a while. When I couldn't take it anymore, I knocked on the door with my knuckle. Tap tap tap. "When you're done . . . I'll be in the car," I said as calmly as I could.

Emily spit out two or three more epithets that had my name attached to them, walked out of her room wearing her pretty Laura Ashley going-to-church dress, shot me a satisfied look, and held the apartment door for me as we left. Clearly, she thought she had won that round. I agreed.

Once I took it upon myself to assume responsibility for Emily's devastation over our move, she and I settled into a teary truce. We spent several months saying a very long good-bye to our home, clinging to the places and friendships that had sustained us over twelve years. I lingered at Little Folks School, absorbing for the last time the grand lessons that working with toddlers had taught me: to be in the moment, to play with abandon, to nap when you need to, and to preserve your friendships by saying "I'm sorry" when necessary.

The moving van came on the last day of June. I rented a smaller panel van and decided to drive Emily and the cat and some of our possessions to Chicago. After running out of boxes, we stuffed our things into garbage bags and threw them into the van. That's when I realized the essential truth about garbage bags. Anything put into a garbage bag, no matter how precious, has a way of becoming garbage once it's in the bag. We looked like we were headed for the landfill. The very last thing we grabbed from our apartment before closing the door was the emergency stash of Twizzlers, pretzels, and Friskies I'd placed in a suitcase the year before. This symbol of my anxiety would sustain us during the drive.

Our exit from Washington was as inglorious, poignant,

and full of hope as our arrival had been, exactly twelve years before. That night we smuggled the cat into a motel in Ohio. The following evening we pulled onto an overpass on the outskirts of Chicago and got our first look at its muscular skyline. Far away, high over the center of our new city, Independence Day fireworks bloomed in great bursts. Chicago was throwing a grand party, and we assumed it was intended just for us.

EIGHT

Playing Hearts

Dating in the Age of Dread

O NE OF MY grander dreams when changing cities
was to mix up and revive my dating life. I'd never
had much of a dating life, but in Chicago I decided I would become new and improved. I would be better groomed. I'd be more of a "listener." Maybe I would
go to "clubs" and take up "dancing." I would get contact
lenses, wear boots with heels in the wintertime, get a decent haircut, and in general work harder to be attractive. I
had never worked at all at being attractive, so working
harder didn't involve a lot of effort, which made it easy to
commit to the concept.

I got the haircut and the contacts. I even submitted to a

brow and lip wax that left me with red welts in the shape of a Groucho Marx unibrow and mustache. I went home and applied ice to my face, and once the swelling went down, Emily and I decided that I had taken baby steps in the right direction.

Most significantly, Chicago had rolled out the red carpet for me. For a month or so, I was everywhere—on the *Today* show and *CBS Sunday Morning*, featured in newspaper advertisements and in a series of radio ads where I talked about my new high-profile job. A week after I'd started writing the "Ask Amy" column, Emily and I took a cab home from the office. The driver looked in the rearview mirror at us and then did a double take. "You're that advice person! You're 'Ask Amy'!" he said.

"But you can call me 'Ask,'" I said.

Emily and I ran into our apartment, laughing.

"Mom—you're famous!"

"Jeez, now I wonder if I should have given him a bigger tip. I mean, I bet Barbara Walters is a big tipper."

"And Kelly Ripa," Emily added, helpfully.

The quick flash of local celebrity supplemented my new eyebrows nicely, and for the first time in recent memory, boys started to call.

Despite all of my experience to the contrary, I have always maintained a very optimistic outlook about my romantic prospects—especially during those long dry spells when I haven't been out much. For me, dating is a lot like going to a professional baseball game—it's an activity that always seems better in the abstract. I get very excited, for instance, at the prospect of watching the Chicago Cubs play, but once I get to Wrigley Field and have that first hot dog and beer, I'm usually ready to go home. Pretty quickly, the players—like my many blind dates, first dates, future prospects, and near misses—start to blend together, and I wonder what's on TV.

My first Chicago date seemed promising—as all of my dates do before I have them. This was a person, let's call him "Leif," who I rejected (and though other details have been forgotten, I remember this with complete clarity) because of the lettuce.

I was first introduced to Leif just after I started my new job, when he cold-called my office and told me that we knew some people in common. We had a brief "getting-to-know-you" chat on the phone, and he invited me to lunch. This was a nice development. In the vision I had of my new Chicago dating life, I would be having lunch with nice gentlemen who called me up and invited me out.

Before meeting Leif in person I was, as usual, extremely excited and optimistic about the outcome. I Googled him and read some of his work. I was happy to learn that though he was a lawyer, he was the good kind—not the Washington lobbyist type I'd met in DC, but a Chicago sort of lawyer who actually helped people in ways that I was sure would be revealed with passionate sensitivity when we met.

I also Google-imaged him and liked his looks. He wore little rimless Trotsky glasses that seemed the perfect accessory to his old-school liberal politics. I pictured him wearing his little glasses and handing out food and green cards to masses of immigrants down at the Chicago stockyards.

I accessed the *Chicago Tribune*'s database and read stories mentioning him. This I did for an entire afternoon. When I ran into one of the colleagues Leif had mentioned to me on the phone, I told her that Leif and I were going to meet for lunch. "Oh, Leif?" She gave a knowing little chuckle. "He goes out with everybody. Going out with Leif is like a rite of passage when you first move here. I went out with him myself in the 1980s, before I was married," she said. This didn't sit particularly well, but I decided that even if Leif wasn't a keeper, perhaps dating him was like doing a short tour in the minor leagues. Dating him would polish me up for *the show*. I called my friend Gay and told her about him. I also called my friend Margaret and told her about him. Then I called my friend Nancy, Rachel, and my mother and told them all about him.

We met at an old-timey downtown deli/lunch joint—the kind of place that has been around forever, with older waitresses and a faithful clientele. The first thing I noticed was that he was thin as a celery stalk. I wondered if he was a smoker, though he had good coloring. Maybe he was an ultramarathoner. We made our way to a table. I told Leif I loved the choice of restaurants and he explained that it was a classic old Chicago place famous for its schnitzel, cabbage rolls, and sauerkraut.

We looked at the menu and the waitress came over. I was trying to decide between the weiner schnitzel and the mixed grill sausage plate with German potato salad, so I asked him to order first.

"Do you have a clear broth? Like a chicken soup, but without any noodles—oh, and no matzoh ball?"

The waitress had a thick Polish accent. She sighed. "Sure, OK on that. Anything else?"

"Salad. I'd love one of those small salads, but no mushrooms or green peppers. And do you use regular-size tomatoes or cherry tomatoes? Never mind, I don't want any tomatoes at all. Really, just the lettuce in a bowl. What kind of dressing do you have? Actually, I'll just stick with vinegar. Just the lettuce and vinegar."

The waitress looked at me.

"Wow—it's sort of like having lunch with Meg Ryan—you know, from *When Harry Met Sally*," I said to her.

Leif interjected, "*She* doesn't know what you're talking about," he said, gesturing toward the waitress.

"Sure I do. Meg Ryan can't ever order off the menu, just like you," she said.

I decided to go with the open-faced grilled Polish sausage sandwich with peppers and onions. I also ordered a chocolate shake and knew from the first slurp that I could never like someone thinner than I am who wouldn't give a waitress credit for knowing about a classic movie that is, after all, sort of all about ordering food and pickiness.

Leif called once after our lunch. As I listened to his message on my office voice mail, I worried that I had been overly picky and hard on Leif, but then I thought about the lettuce and disliked him all over again. I didn't return the call, and he never called again.

Jack was a prominent Chicago businessman. I received a charming letter from his daughter at the office. "You don't know me, but I'm a fan of yours and I understand that you're single," she started. She had me, of course, at the "fan" part. She went on to say that her father, a delightful and handsome prominent businessman, had just gotten divorced after his very long marriage to her mother. The daughter was now contacting me to ask if I'd like to go out with her dad.

The letter from the daughter fixing me up with her dad had all sorts of appealing *Sleepless in Seattle* overtones, though the daughter mentioned that she was a thirty-year-old registered nurse and thus a little tall for this particular pimping theme park ride. All the same, I thought that this was the ultimate "meet-cute." I was already writing the *New York Times* "Vows" column in my head. I contacted her and said that her father could e-mail me at the office. He did so, and he was the right amount of charming and embarrassed. We agreed to meet.

I need to state for the record that I'd rather date a rodeo clown than someone who describes himself as a prominent businessman. Businessmen don't seem to go for me, either. I have already aged out of their eye-candy fantasies, and I can tell that sometimes I remind them of their ex-wives. However, one characteristic of my dating life is my ongoing desire to switch it up, to abandon what doesn't work and try new things—unfortunately all the while falling into the same old patterns.

We met at a hotel bar.

Jack PowerPoint-ed me through his many accomplishments, presenting them as bullet points along the straight and narrow pathway that was his life. He was proud of the fact that he had never as much as tasted alcohol. "How come?" I asked, ordering another.

He said he didn't like it. "But if you've never tasted it, how do you know you don't like it?" I asked.

"I just know," he said.

Jack went on to describe his heartbreak at the ending of his long marriage and his surprise at the fact that he was something of a babe magnet. One of his neighbors was interested in him and they had had a fling, but he was really confused, even though she had great legs. Also—he was thinking of entering politics. Having just moved from Washington, where everybody is thinking of entering or leaving politics, I felt like this was something we could really talk about. I asked him why he was interested in politics.

The expression on his face was just like the one Teddy Kennedy gave to Roger Mudd in 1980 when Kennedy was running for president and Roger Mudd inadvertently torpedoed the candidate's presidential aspirations by asking the most obvious question, "Why do you want to be president?" Jack looked like he had just woken from a deep sleep in a strange hotel room. Like he'd lost his bearings.

While he was thinking of an answer, I excused myself and went to the ladies' room. I called Emily from the stall and told her that if this thing wrapped up soon, we'd be able to make it to the movies for the early show and then we could have dinner after.

"Is it that bad?" she asked.

"Yeah, it's pretty bad. I mean it's not bad bad, it's just not good."

"Ugh. Boys!" she said.

Soon after I got back to the table, my phone rang. It was Emily. I could hear her switching TV channels in a rhythmic, bored fashion.

"Hey, Mom, it's me—your daughter. Um . . . I think I sprained my ankle. Ouch, it really hurts."

"Oh no, honey—are you OK?" I said. *"Sorry, it's my daughter . . ."* I gestured to Jack.

"Oh—wait. I might have swallowed some poison by accident. Do you know the number for poison control?"

"Emily, I'm in the middle of something. I can't—yes, that's not good. OK. I'll be home in a few minutes." I sighed.

"I'm going to take the 151 bus and I'll meet you at the place near the theater," she said before hanging up.

My rendezvous with the prominent businessman had run its course. I turned to him. "Sorry, I've got to go. It seems that my daughter needs me to come home. It was nice meeting you and good luck!" Emily and I met at the movies and I realized yet again that I would rather be on a date with my daughter than just about anybody I could imagine.

Later the prominent businessman did run for public office, repeatedly, giving many thousands of people the opportunity to vote for someone else.

My first dating experiences right after my divorce didn't go well. Some of my later dating experiences also haven't gone well, but for different reasons. I cried about my divorce on the very first postdivorce date—a blind date fix-up with a Washington lawyer. After I stopped crying he told me he had a great therapist who had helped him get through his own divorce. I was too embarrassed to see the guy again, though I did book an appointment with his therapist.

My second dating experience was with an architect. Yum, I thought, an architect. I could definitely see myself with an architect. I loved the idea of being with someone who had to occasionally go out to "job sites" and wear a hard hat but who wasn't a teamster. The architect said he was really into judo and he hated his ex-wife, who was turning his children against him. Even though I didn't even like the architect, I had already decided to sleep with him if I got the chance. The architect eventually rejected me for structural reasons. His exact words were, "I don't like your body." Despite this harsh assessment, he called me a few weeks later. "I'm at my Men in Anger workshop up the street and wonder if you want to have a drink after I'm done?" he asked.

"Well, what are the Men in Anger angry about?" I asked him, though I was pretty sure I already knew the answer.

"Women," he said.

I decided to pass.

The rejection on structural issues prompted me to pull away from dating for a long time, establishing a pattern that persists to this day: I engage in little flurries of dating, followed by long periods of happily not dating. The alone periods aren't because I am necessarily disgusted with my choices or prospects, but more because I'm tired. Meeting and getting to know new people is exhausting, but then being alone or lonely is tiring too.

When Emily was little, my inconsistent dating habits worked well with our family life. I got a babysitter if I wanted to go out and didn't involve or introduce her to anyone I was interested in. The last thing I ever wanted to do was try to explain or defend my personal choices or convey my romantic disappointment to the kid. I also didn't want her to get a glimpse into the sausage factory that is my romantic life.

Once I'd recovered from the architect, I went through a phase of fantasizing about and then dating guys I'd known in college. This lasted for several years because I went to a pretty big school and there were several interesting candidates. A couple of these experiences actually turned into relationships of sorts. There was a lawyer (again) in New York City and a screenwriter in Los Angeles. The lawyer was a cutie-pie. For several months, I would go out with him every month or so when I took Emily to New York to see her father (my ex had married his girlfriend and moved to Manhattan). The longer I knew him, however, the more remote he became. He seemed to experience a reverse tele-scoping scale of affection. As we grew closer, he became fidgety and fussy. He told me we would never have sex. I liked him enough that I was considering having a forever-chaste romance with him, but finally he seemed to more or less disappear, and I didn't have any choice but to let him vanish. He was like melting snow, gone in stages by spring.

The experience with the screenwriter took longer to cycle through. At the beginning, it had the makings of a grand passion, but it turned out that we were both just act-ing in separate movie romances. Mine was a Busby Berke-ley musical. His was *The Bipolar Express*, directed by Quentin Tarantino. He told me he had been engaged several times but couldn't figure out why he'd never gotten married. One thing or another always went wrong.

A clue that I was in trouble was when he asked me to marry him on our first meeting. Then he flew to Washing-ton and asked me to marry him on our second meeting. This sort of behavior sounds better on paper than it is in real life. On paper it's the sort of cute anecdote you think you're going to tell your eventual grandchildren. In real life it's menacing. Years later, after we had become friends again, he told me that he was a blackout drunk during that period of his life.

Much of my dating life has been little more than a series of glancing connections and clashing agendas. He's ready but I'm not. I'm ready but he's not interested. He's interested but I don't like him. I'm crazy about him but he's with somebody else. I don't like his attitude toward children. He doesn't like my career. I chase him down the street, he hides in an alley.

Take "Sven." Sven was five years younger. He liked adventure travel, and I liked him. He lived in New York, and on a trip there I called him and we went out to dinner. There was a lot of verbal cleverness. We kissed on the street, and I liked that very much. After many weeks of back-and-forth, we spent a romantic evening together, and then the next day he asked me to meet him for coffee. He asked what I thought of him. As in, "What do you think of me and what do you want from this relationship?" I said, "Well, I think you're great and I'm in." "You're in?" he asked. "Yes, I'm in. Like in kickball when you pick sides. I'm on your side."

"I know a secret about you. You're actually *nice*," he said.

I remember telling him that I felt that life was too short to spend it wondering what people think of us. "So yes, I do like you. And yes, I am actually nice. But don't tell anybody and *please* don't screw this up," I said.

Two weeks later I learned that Sven was going on an

adventure vacation with his former girlfriend. "I don't really know what it means," he said to me on the phone. But I knew what it meant, and I was out.

Girlfriends and sisters are the best part of dating. They will spend hours decoding dates, reviewing them in a moment-by-moment timeline. They will ask you what you wore and if you were having a good hair date. They will ask for a verbatim account of what he said and what you said. They will ask if you kissed, pecked, hugged, shook hands, or ran off screaming into the night at the end of the date. They will listen in as you replay his cell phone message twenty times, and they will comment on the attractive timbre of his voice. "Oh, he sounds cute, play it again!" they'll say. They will fret with you as you decide whether or not the message was merely a polite check-in call or an invitation to call back. They will help you to decide to call him back and then five minutes later they will say, "You know, I've been thinking about it, I don't think you should call. Let him make another move."

After a strange little spate of going out with three men in a row I was fairly certain were gay, I brought my mother into the conversation. I had just told her about my most recent date, attending a stage production of *Kiss of the Spider Woman* with a guy from my church. From the opening curtain I knew he was gay, but I couldn't tell if he knew it; I certainly didn't want to be the one to tell him.

I was standing in my mother's kitchen. "But why on earth would a gay man want to date me?" I asked her.

"Think about it, Amy. You're pleasant, you're present-able, and you love musical theater. What's not to like? You're a catch!" she said.

As Emily has gotten older, she's also entered my dating team as a consultant. Her willing participation in some of my various minifiascos is proof that if you wait long enough, even your children will try to get you out of the house. Emily's specialty, she likes to think, is gauging suitability. And if she's not sure, she has been known to pull out a Ouija board or Magic 8 Ball for confirmation. "Sorry, Mom—it says, 'Outlook not so good.'"

The women in my life say things like, "Well, I think if you really wanted a guy, you'd probably have one." This is pro-vocative. It sounds true, but it's not. They will also say, "As soon as you stop looking, he'll appear." Then they say, "You just have to get out there. Take a polka class. You're never go-ing to meet someone in your living room." After that they say, "You'll find someone when you least expect it."

I have taken all of this to heart, and I have spent years looking, not looking, expecting, not expecting, being pro-active, making phone calls, admitting to crushes, denying attractions, and leaving it up to the Universe. None of this works. But it all works. The search for connection is the most basic and beautiful impulse I have. I try to enjoy my efforts—even when they are misguided, not reciprocated, or doofus in the extreme. I try to remember this when my romantic pursuits make me sob over the sink or—even worse—when they lead to a series of Match.com coffee dates that blend together like a giant decaffeinated mochaccino mess.

Several years ago, Emily and I were in Freeville over Christmas. It was a Saturday night, and my mother and aunties were gathering next door at my aunt Millie's house. We were going to play hearts. Emily headed over to Aunt Millie's house a little ahead of me—I stayed behind to feed the cat.

It was a beautiful night—inky and cold. Several inches of snow had fallen during the day, and when I looked up at the streetlights along Main Street, snowflakes seemed suspended—frozen in place in the cold air. As I walked along the sidewalk toward Millie's house, a man walked toward me. As we passed, I said, "Hello," and he looked up.

It was unmistakably Brian, the love of my young life. I hadn't seen him in twenty-five years, but except for his silver hair, he looked exactly the same.

"Oh my God, what are you doing here?" I asked him.

"I was looking for you," he said.

Brian told me that he had parked his car at the end of Main Street and had decided to walk down the street and see if he could find me. He had no idea that I had a house in Freeville—the last he knew, I was in Washington. But he remembered where Aunt Millie lived and said he had decided to walk past.

I asked Brian to come with me to Millie's. When I walked in with him, everyone was thrilled. Of any of the men in my life, including the one I eventually married,

Brian was my family's sentimental favorite. He was good, he was kind, and he loved me. We were high school sweethearts, and even though we went to different colleges and agreed to see other people, we stayed in touch and would occasionally see each other on our school vacations. Brian went into the Peace Corps after college, and we exchanged sweet and sentimental letters. When he got out of the Peace Corps, he flew directly to Washington and came to see me. At that point I hadn't seen him in two years.

Twenty-five years ago, we stood on a street corner in Washington and I told Brian that I had someone else in my life. This was the man who, after a tempestuous relationship of many years, would marry and then leave me. That day, Brian got into a cab. I was so relieved to be rid of him that I didn't even invest the time necessary to watch him ride away, and to this day, I don't think I've ever been more cruel.

Brian sat with us in Aunt Millie's living room and told us about his wife and their two children. He was a schoolteacher, and they lived in Florida. Both of his children played the violin for the youth orchestra. Their family had just come back from a trip to Ireland on a Celtic music tour. He showed us pictures, and they were lovely. He asked Emily questions about school and wondered whether she liked to ski and ice-skate. He was only in town for the weekend because he was moving his mother into a nursing home in Florida and he had come to get her.

I walked Brian to his car and sat in the front seat with him while it warmed up. I asked if he had heard about my divorce, and he said he had. "I know that all those years ago, I took five minutes out of my day to break up with you, but I want you to know that that's exactly what my husband did to me. Trust me, I can imagine how that must have felt and I feel like the least I can do is apologize to you now. You're too nice a person to enjoy that, but I wanted you to know."

"I can enjoy it a little bit, Amy," he said. We hugged, I sniffled, and we said good-bye. This time I watched him until he was out of sight.

I walked back down Main Street, retracing the snow trail our boots had left, and went to my aunt's house to re-trieve Emily and tell her the story. I wanted her to know about the karmic wheel of romance, about how the things you say and do now will revisit you over and over again. I told her that the feelings she has when she is young will be the same feelings when she's old, and that she should try not to be afraid of them. I wanted her to be bold with her choices but careful in her actions. I told her never to be mean to someone who loved her, because regret is the only true casualty of love.

Last year Emily told me that she wanted to invite a boy to the prom. My heart sank. I was afraid that in the super-charged atmosphere of high school at prom time, she would see her crush crushed. I wasn't ready for her to face the rejection that often follows when you make your desires known. But the boy said yes. He came to our house beforehand and gave her a corsage and cheerfully submitted to photographs. I was delighted to see that Emily evidently had excellent taste in the opposite sex. Then I took to my bed with anxiety. The phone rang at 2 A.M. I could barely hear my daughter's voice over the music.

"I'm having a great time!" she shouted, and I thought, Well, here we go.

NINE

The Apex of Dorkitude

Dork, Like Me

A S EMILY SLID into her teen years I was made aware—almost daily—of how *easy* she was. Some of my friends who had teenagers had all but given up on actually raising them. Their goal was to survive, to shut their eyes and simply wait it out. I couldn't blame them—given even the normal developmental teenage trials (lying, drinking, ramming around in cars), I would have done exactly the same thing.

Emily wasn't like these teenagers or the ones we saw on television, however. She was the kid who got a cell phone but rarely used it. She wasn't overly interested in fashion, driving, or dating. Overall, she was pretty nice to me.

I could only take credit for this much—I had done my best. I had raised her to care about my welfare just as I cared about hers.

But I knew something else about her, and this, probably more than any other factor, made my daughter the girl she was.

Emily hadn't just inherited my dark eyes and low forehead; she had also inherited another family trait: complete and utter dorkitude. Dorkitude can emerge at any time in a child's development, but with Emily I first recognized the signs when she was in kindergarten.

I used to watch them on the playground—the five-year-olds headed toward coolness. The boys had last names as first names: Carter, Simpson, and Bailey. Their moms dressed them in tiny leather aviator jackets and blue jeans. They were the lords of the seesaw and the kings of the jungle gym. The girls—all Taylors and Haleys—wore leggings, sweaters, and size two plastic clogs, which they somehow knew how to run in without falling. They hung in clusters near the swing set, teaching one another the dark art of playground gossip.

After scanning the play structures for Emily, I would almost always find her near the base of a large tree, playing with the handful of kids who had no kingdom. These were the stateless kindergarten refugees trying to create their own world out of the leftovers.

Emily would see me and run over to the fence. "What are you doing?" I'd ask.

"Pretending."

"What are you pretending?"

"We're pretending to be dogs."

Emily pretended to be a dog for over a year. Then she pretended to be a florist.

Somehow, when it came time to collect the gamine beauty, the athletic prowess, the competitive and aggressive ballet dancing/ice-skating/kung fu talent that children these days absolutely must possess, my daughter and I were waiting in line for the bus to the public library.

Every year on Emily's birthday we had a party in our apartment building for the handful of girls she liked the most. Emily was the only kid in her crew who lived in an apartment—the other kids lived in "real houses" with driveways and front lawns and had one of each parent: one mom and one dad. Their own birthday parties were festivals of fun, often featuring a popular ballerina-clown for hire who went by the name Princess Patty and whose act involved dancing, magic wands, fairy dust, dress up, and makeovers. Princess Patty gave me the creeps, mainly because she wore bright red circles of rouge on each cheek and talked in a squeaky voice, making her sound as if she were hopped up on helium.

For Emily's eighth birthday we had cake in our living room, and then I took all of the kids on the Metro down to the National Mall and went to the planetarium. I was surprised at how few of the kids had traveled around town on the train or had visited the tourist destinations on the Mall.

The Mall was where Emily and I went to ice-skate and ride the Victorian carousel on Fridays. It was where we went after touring the Capitol building or the National Gallery for the umpteenth time. We considered it to be our own front lawn.

After the planetarium show, I brought the girls back to our apartment. While we were waiting for their parents to pick them up I asked them to tell me what they wanted to be when they grew up. Reflecting the high-flying careerist hopes of their parents, they weighed in with their well-considered choices. Hannah wanted to be a movie star. Caroline was considering a career as a diplomat. Elizabeth was thinking about being an economist, but she wasn't sure yet; she was also considering running for Congress. Isabel wanted to be a plastic surgeon—not one of those plastic surgeons who just does nose jobs, but the kind who goes to the Dominican Republic and fixes kids with facial deformities, she pointed out.

We came around to Emily—the birthday girl and last in the group.

"I want to be an optometrist and sell eyeglass frames in a shop," she said.

I've been a dork for a long, long time. An aggressive strain seems to run through our family, infecting random members with the desire to be contra dancers, sing madrigals, and join the AV club. We don't have math or science smarts, so unfortunately in our clan the dork-trait most often publicly manifests itself not by excelling at academic subjects but by singing Elizabethan music and strolling—while wearing a very unfortunate costume.

I actually made it all the way through high school thinking that I had escaped the family curse. I played sports, got the lead in the school plays, was a good student, a cheerleader, and the vice president of everything. Then in college, I noticed the signs of sudden and advanced dorkitude when, quite of my own volition, I joined the university's madrigal choir. Unfortunately, our debut performance was on the same night I was supposed to go out with a guy I was dying to get to know better. Rather than preserving my self-esteem by rescheduling the date, I took him to the student union—our performance venue—and just after our first beer, said, "Um, I'll be right back." A few minutes later, like a superhero descending from Mount Dorktopolis, I emerged from the bathroom wearing a velvet cape and mop cap and stood with the rest of the similarly costumed group under a prop Victorian lamppost, singing, "Hey nonni nonni." We then strolled, arm in arm, in circles around the small room.

Emily, who had a 50 percent chance of being normal like her father, manifested early onset—presumably because I was raising her. Symptoms included an acute interest in books and reading, musical talent, the desire to go to museums, and the inability to either throw or catch a ball. I compounded matters by refusing to expose her to the same media most other children enjoyed. She was raised on NPR and old movies—mainly because that's what I like. I understood the impact of this choice when I heard four-year-old Emily imitating Terry Gross one day from her booster seat in the back of the car. "Hi, I'm Terry Gross, and this is . . . Fresh Air-r-r-r-e," she said, drawing out the last word in a breathy way that I realized was exactly as the radio host did. One Halloween, the same year all the other kids seemed to be Power Rangers and Powerpuff Girls, Emily chose to dress up as Laura Ingalls Wilder, complete with a bonnet and accented by her own prop—a wooden spoon.

Like the rest of her dorkitudinous clan, Emily was happily unself-conscious about her character trait. This was a huge relief to me because it meant that my young daughter would willingly accompany me to a one-man show celebrating the life of Noël Coward, a documentary about Nazis living in Brazil, an evening of Gilbert and Sullivan, and, it turned out, Bill Clinton's impeachment hearings. As I explained it to her, if you have a choice between going to a regular Thursday in fourth grade and attending the historic impeachment hearings of the forty-second president, it's pretty simple—you should choose to attend the hearings, and of course she did.

Middle school is hard enough for any girl, but Emily returned to school from vacation having to tell her friends that her mom took her to the National Storytelling Festival in Jonesborough, Tennessee, instead of to Disney World or the beach. She also bore the shame of never having shopped at The Limited. Fortunately for Emily, her sense of herself seemed to inoculate her from the worst slings and arrows of adolescence. She excelled at finding kids to befriend and had great taste in people, even in the terrible minefield of seventh grade. She seemed able to spot a "mean girl" at a great distance and, using an exchange student as a human shield, would make her way to clarinet practice or off to choir. She won a coveted spot in the Washington Children's Choir, and I was relieved to see her thrown together at rehearsals twice a week with those of her kind—the smart kids with quirky personalities who never got the memo that they weren't cool.

Emily's quirkiness served her well when she was entering ninth grade and had to change cities and start at a new school. She never seemed to worry about fitting in because she never assumed that she would. She quickly found her home, participating in theater and music at her school, and we explored new museums, discovered the opera, and found movie theaters to go to together.

Fortunately, Emily's school in Chicago was small and easy to navigate. The madrigal choir found her in no time. This choir had costumes, loads of costumes—and not just the matchy-matchy uniforms she was used to in Washington, but gowns made of velvet with contrasting bodices trimmed in braid. The boys wore doublets and knickers, puffy-sleeved pirate shirts, and pointy velvet hats that looked vaguely ecclesiastical, like something the pope might wear on vacation. Emily told me that at least a few of the boys were reduced to wearing their mothers' panty hose under their knickers.

It was Emily who first called the near tragedy that befell her madrigal choir the Apex of Dorkitude, though I worried that declaring something to be an apex at such a tender age might set a person up for disappointment later. We have examined the evidence, however. We've run it through the lab, called in the forensics team, and have concluded that what happened on the stage of the Frances Parker School in Chicago that soft spring night in Emily's junior year of high school was without question a turning point, the fulcrum on which her character teetered and was tested.

The madrigal choir was having a dress rehearsal in preparation for their spring concert, to be held the following night. A handful of parents had gathered in the large auditorium to watch the twenty or so kids run through their numbers. The kids strolled onto the school's stage dressed in their velvet frippery, looking like they'd escaped from a bus and truck show of *Kiss Me, Kate*. Emily, the tallest of the group, towered over the tenors—a knot of tiny ninth grade boys still waiting for their voice change and accompanying facial hair.

The group clumped in together in the center of the stage and started to sing. Swaying occurred. Many of the kids looked uncomfortable; they tugged at their gowns and brocade vests as their eyes conveyed their mortification at their predicament. The soprano section, accustomed as they were to going through life wearing belly shirts, miniskirts and UGG boots, looked like they wished the earth would open up and swallow them whole. (I assumed their parents had made them join the group to pad their high school résumés.) Emily was placed in the back of the group, next to a super-size boy baritone. I noticed that she looked completely at ease in her blue gown and slippers, and ever so slightly in love with herself. She was simply singing, and the music was doing what music does—it was taking her someplace. Watching from my seat in the auditorium, I couldn't help but reflect that my girl had what appeared to be complete immunity from the desires of the herd.

I could see Emily's future spinning out like an old-timey film strip: she would read textbooks for pleasure. She would laugh loudly at her own jokes. She would in all likelihood attend a Tolkien convention. She would go to a costume party dressed as a Wookiee. She would leave at least one ladies' room during a blind date with a trail of toilet paper stuck to her shoe. When true love hit, she would punctuate the moment by vomiting. There would be an episode of driving through town with a bag of groceries resting on the hood of her car while passersby waved and hollered. My daughter would lead a singular life. I said a little prayer to the God of Normalcy that it would also be joyful.

The group was singing their first chorus of "So Well I Know Who's Happy" when I heard a cracking sound. One board of the stage had splintered and was starting to buckle. Like a paramecium inching across a microscope slide, the group angled and shifted as one organism, moving slightly stage right and, prompted by their conductor, continued to sing.

So well I know who's happy
Too well I know who's happy
Fa la la la
La la la la la la la

That's when the old wooden stage decided it could no longer contain this teen collection of velvet and harmony. Out of nowhere and with the swiftness of a lightning strike a crater the size of a Buick opened in the stage. Singers fell sideways and backward—arms flying, velvet billowing—and were swallowed in quick succession into a four-foot-deep sinkhole. Three legs and feet—one wearing a sneaker and two in slippers—remained above the stage line. They waved upside down briefly before disappearing.

Witnesses to natural disasters always note how quickly they happen. That's because disasters, like good romances, contain the element of surprise. For a moment, I wondered if the sopranos had gotten their wish. Could teen mortification actually be potent enough to violate the space/time continuum? Did they create a vortex of sorts, carrying the group back in time to the 1600s and placing them in a small town in Derbyshire—where they would finally realize their dream of fitting in?

I was the first parent to the stage. I stood at the edge of the great hole and looked down into it. It was a scene of velvet carnage—a jumble of seemingly unrelated legs and torsos. Gowns were flipped over heads. Puffy sleeves had caught the air and like balloons expanded to their full size.

I heard soft moaning but otherwise the group was alarmingly quiet. The school's janitor joined me, and we started to pull out the sopranos. Though they seemed basically unhurt, the moment they tasted freedom, the girls of the section checked their hair and then choked with sobs as they ran to their parents in the audience, some of whom seemed to be already phoning their lawyers. I saw many therapy sessions in their future. ("Doctor, what does it mean? Last night I had that dream about the tuning fork again. And I seem to have developed an irrational fear of brocade.")

One by one we pulled the kids out of the pit and sent them limping off to their parents' embrace. Miraculously, no one seemed seriously hurt; ironically, it was probably the acres of velvet that broke their fall and spared them from physical (if not psychic) injury. Emily was on the very bottom of the scrum, under a pint-size tenor who was splayed on top of her. His panty hose were ripped, and his knee was a little bloody. He sheepishly brushed back a tear as we helped him out. I looked down at Emily. She was a big velvet **X** on the floor. Silently, she sat and then stood up, brushed a piece of flooring from her skirt, and held her arms aloft to be hoisted out. Once on the lip of the stage crater, she looked out at the assemblage—by now there was a small crowd, including the head of the school and half of the basketball team—and then looked at me.

I scanned her lovely face. I was ready to jolly her along and prop her up in the way I'd been doing off and on her whole life. I was preparing to seize this teachable moment, even though I couldn't quite arrive at the proper lesson. I wondered how much it bothered her that I'd yanked her from Washington to Chicago, forcing her to engage in the exhausting and often fruitless ritual of trying to be somebody in a new high school. Emily had heard my story about when I took a date to my college madrigal performance at the student union—what I didn't think I'd told her was that the boy in question was her father. I wanted her to know that sometimes people love you despite your dorkitude—and sometimes, if you're really lucky, they love you *because* of it. I thought of my own greatest hits of embarrassment, like the time at a wedding last spring when I reached into my coat pocket for a pen in order to write down my phone number for a guy and, instead of a pen, pulled out a tampon. What I wanted to tell her was . . . you get used to it.

"Well, *that* happened," Emily said, as if she had spent her lifetime expecting exactly this and now she could cross it off her life list of humiliations. Then she gave a little bow. There was a scatter of applause. Then she laughed. Of everyone in the large room, she was the only person laughing.

That night the outer envelope of the dorkdom galaxy was stretched tight. Emily punched a hole through it and Chuck Yeagered her way to the other side. And—violating her family's predisposition, her upbringing, and the expectations of the rest of the world—she came out cool.

TEN

The Marrying Man

M Y FATHER CALLED me one day last summer. "Um, it's your father. I shot a bear and now it looks like I've got to go to court."

I replayed his message a few times. Emily and I stood in the kitchen next to the answering machine, idly looking at each other as we listened. His voice was nasal and gravelly and his accent full of flatness and diphthongs. I hadn't heard it in a long time. He asked me to call back and left his number.

Emily didn't have a relationship with her grandfather. Though she had met him a handful of times, these encounters were glancing. I didn't really have a relationship with him, either; my father and I were passively engaged in what a social scientist would probably call a "benevolent estrangement." After years of feeling bad about him for abandoning our family, followed by more years of fearing that I would make similar choices, I had come to realize that though he and I shared some familial traits—a head of thick hair, the set and shape of our eyes, a fondness for farm equipment, and a tendency to dominate conversations—we had opposite predilections. He liked to leave; I liked to stay. His pattern was to be in touch once or twice a year, always during the summer when he would drive through Freeville unannounced, randomly stopping at his children's houses—most often when I didn't happen to be home. In many years of living in Freeville during the summer, I had come to regard my father as a sort of exotic summer crop, like a gourd that ripens only when you're not there to see it. This summertime phone call was my first-ever phone message from him.

I dialed his number. His wife, Pat, answered. I realized I had forgotten her name, so I just introduced myself and asked for my father. "He's out back with his bees, but I'll call him," she said. I heard her Marjorie Main voice sail out the back door. "Charrr-illlllls!!!" I had never heard him called Charles before—it was a bit of a surprise. Back when I knew him, everyone called him Buck, the nickname his mother gave him because he was so jumpy as a child. He was so energetic, he couldn't sit still, just like a buck, the story went. I think of bucks as being majestic, many-antlered royalty of the woods, so his nickname never quite made sense to me until I realized that the reference was most likely not to a buck, but to a bucking bronco. Regardless, his nickname suited him. It is the name of someone who doesn't want to be a Charles.

My parents were married for twenty-two years. My three siblings and I spent the bulk of our childhoods on our crumbling dairy farm of a hundred acres on Mill Street—just beyond the Freeville village limits. Now in the summers since Emily and I took up seasonal residency on Main Street, we would occasionally take our kayaks out behind our house and float down Fall Creek, which took us past the farmhouse and scruffy pastureland of my childhood home. It is nothing to look at—this parcel of land bisected by an unruly creek—yet this little patch of my childhood regularly brings tears to my eyes. I love it beyond my understanding.

I have a persistent vision of my father making his way across the field in back of our barn. Going somewhere! His step was springy and enterprising. He drew his bucket from a bottomless well of energy and cultivated a tough restlessness that got him into trouble. He loved shortcuts and windfalls and wayward moneymaking projects, sometimes involving other men such as himself, who, when things went sour, tended to punch each other in the nose. He was full of loud bluster and profanity. He cast himself as a government-hating athletic iconoclast. He was exciting. He was handsome like a B movie star, in the manner of Glenn Ford, but with the ego of a Caribbean despot. I loved to watch him but not, I think, in the way daughters commonly love to look at their fathers. He was like an animal. Unpredictable. He would crouch beside the belligerent Holsteins in our barn during the evening milking, a hand-rolled cigarette between his lips, cursing the cows and barking orders at his team of assistants—his three disinterested daughters and silent son. Rachel, Anne, and I were more consumed by practicing cheerleading jumps on the concrete alley between the rows of cows than in being "milkmaids," which is how our father sometimes referred to us.

Our brother, Charlie, was having a Led Zeppelin teenhood. He did as he was told with a sort of moody indifference, but sometimes it was all he could do to keep up with our father's barked orders, what with the lyrics to "Whole Lotta Love" coursing through his head. Our father must have suspected early on that his children would not be the Dairy Princesses and Future Farmers of his imaginings, and yet there we all were—in the barn, working.

To make ends meet on our ever-failing farm, my father was also a steelworker. He said he loved the work—he loved being outside and liked to climb and to dangle from the substructure of a building. In between the morning and evening milkings, he spent his days laying iron with Iroquois and Mohawk Indians recruited from nearby reservations. (He liked working with Indian crews, he said, because—like him—they had no fear.)

My father left when I was twelve. It was a sudden thing,

and as far as I know, beyond his travels to increasingly far-off construction jobs, he had given no warning that he would leave home permanently. Our fifty cows were in the field, needing to be milked twice a day. A neighbor helped out in the mornings, and my sisters, brother, and I did the evening milking when we got home from school. Evening chores had often seemed like a warm, antic time. My sisters and I had an understanding that the barnyardlike social rules and pecking order that dominated the rest of our lives in high school stopped at the barn door. Most often Rachel and Anne wouldn't even acknowledge me during an encounter in the hallway at school, but in the barn they treated me almost like a peer—trading school gossip, complaining about their teachers, and teaching me the lyrics to the latest Three Dog Night song we'd been hearing on the radio.

After our father left, our barn became quiet with anxiety. Charlie, only sixteen years old and an indifferent farmer in our father's presence, rose to the occasion as best he could. He handled the heavy lifting while my sisters and I silently went about our business.

We didn't know where Buck was, but after a couple of months he called from Lowville in the North Country. He had taken up with Truck Stop Joan (which was how I snippily thought of her because she worked as a waitress at a roadside diner).

My father told my mother that he had sold our herd of Holsteins. The next day two huge cattle trucks belonging to a larger dairy in Cortland drove in and took the cows away. It was April and raining a cold, hard rain that was washing the last vestiges of dingy snow into the creek. I watched from the driveway as our cows slipped and slid through the mud and were prodded with electric shocks onto the long trucks. They were confused and bleating as they were forced up the ramp and into the dark tunnel of the truck. Even at my relatively young age, I think I knew that dispatching with the cows in such a sudden and cruel fashion was the only scenario that my father could create that I would find truly unforgivable. Sure enough, as an adult, I've attained an emotional stasis about many things, but not about that.

After our cows were gone, I found I missed them terribly. They showed up in my dreams, roaming through my mother's flower beds, lowing quietly and letting me know that we had failed them. Our old red barn was like a cathedral, looming over the landscape of my childhood. It was the size of an ocean liner, with enormous rooms, milking parlors, and lofts. After the cows left, I couldn't go inside it.

The sheriff came to the house, delivering papers to my mother. "Sorry, Jane," he said as he handed her the summons. He looked down at the floor. My father had charged my mother with "cruel and inhuman treatment," which was the only way to get a quick divorce at the time.

We had an auction. The Munson family ran all the auctions in our area, and they handled things. Glenn Munson,

who was a sophomore at our high school, was the auction-
eer. He was born with muscular dystrophy and got around
school in a wheelchair. Glenn's father and uncle hoisted him
onto a platform set up in front of our barn's enormous
doors. He had a microphone hanging around his neck. He
called the auction in a speedy high-pitched singsong auc-
tioneer voice and swayed back and forth like Stevie Wonder
at the piano. Our neighbors bid on our rusty farm implements, milking equipment—even the leftover hay stored in
our barn—and loaded them into their pickups.

My mother and some other women were gathered
around a large coffee urn in the kitchen. They sipped
their coffee and talked in low voices. I told my mother to
come out and see the auction, but she said, "No thanks,
honey." It hadn't occurred to me until that moment that
the public selling of our possessions would be a hard thing
for her to witness. Later in school, whenever Glenn Munson wheeled by in the hallway, I felt him looking at me
compassionately.

The summer after my father left, my brother quit high
school and hitched his way through Scandinavia with a
friend for several months. Then he joined the navy. It was
many years before he came home again. Mom went to work
as a typist at Cornell University.

One night about a year after he left our family, Joan—now
my father's second wife—called. "Where is that bastard?"
she asked. My mother said she didn't know.

My father surfaced again several months later. He had taken up with Jeanne, a formerly close friend of my mother's from many years ago. He was local again. When I was sixteen and playing Zaneeta Shinn in our community production of *The Music Man*, I heard that he was drinking beer at the local bowling alley with some of the older cast members after rehearsals. "He's a riot!" they said. Yeah. He's a scream, I thought.

Buck and Jeanne started moving around. They lived on Long Island for a time while Buck worked construction at the Plum Island Research Facility. They lived in Vermont and Connecticut, where he found work on farms and trimming trees. Then they moved to Port Allegheny, in North Central Pennsylvania. Jeanne was sick for a long time and then died of emphysema. My brother told me she smoked right next to her oxygen canister. He thought she might blow herself up.

When I went to college, my mother left her typing job and went to Cornell as a full-time undergraduate. Then she got her master's degree at Cornell. At fifty-three, she started a teaching career, first at Cornell and later at Ithaca College. She bought herself a nicer coat and carried a briefcase.

An elderly neighbor with no family who lived up the road left his house and all of his property to my mother when he died, and she moved away from the empty farm and resettled up the road in the little place, which was lovely and ghost-free. No ethereal Holsteins roamed the property, and whenever I stayed with her at her new house,

I marveled at the sweet dreams I had while sleeping in the guest room.

My father bought a large old white delivery van, such as laundries use. After Jeanne died, he started driving around. It was as if he was exploring an imaginary sales territory—with himself as the only product. One time during a summertime visit home when Emily was a baby, I was sitting on the porch with my mother when he drove by, slowly. I looked over and saw my father's unmistakable silhouette. "Who's that?" she said. "I think it's my father," I told her. He turned around down the road and came back and drank a cup of coffee with us on the porch. I hadn't seen him in at least ten years, but he was pretty much as I remembered. He was full of optimism, ideas, and schemes involving sure-fire ventures such as fish-farming and emu-raising. He thought he might go to Nova Scotia to pick apples. I pictured him living in his van on the edge of an orchard in Nova Scotia, which turned out to be exactly what he did.

The last few months had been hard on him. While Jeanne was slowly dying, my father had had a small stroke and had a pacemaker installed. After a few days in the hospital, he went AWOL and hitchhiked back to his little house. He opened up the top of his shirt to show me his pacemaker. I could see the outline of a disc the size of a half-dollar sparking away just under the surface of his chest.

I realized that I was relieved that he had left us. All I had to do was look at my mother, the college professor, sitting on the porch in the house that she owned. More than once she'd said that if Buck had stayed, she'd be living in a trailer, and I knew this was true. My father's life tended toward chaos, and he didn't like to be alone.

Six months later, Buck was back from Nova Scotia, once again living in Port Allegheny. He had married again. Her name was Jean. He said he'd met her at church. So far, his wives were named Jane, Joan, Jeanne, and Jean. He had become the often-married protagonist of a George Jones song. Like the old joke goes, I fantasized that if our particular country-and-western song was played backward, the extra wives would fall away one by one, the barn would right itself, the cows would back themselves off the cattle trucks and into the barn, and my father would somehow reverse himself and be the man I remember striding across the field—going somewhere.

One summer day when Emily was nine, I was upstairs when there was a knock on the door. Emily came up to get me. "There's a man at the door," she said. I introduced my father to my daughter. "Emily, this is Buck. My dad," I said. I had told Emily about my dad over the years; as in discussing her own father, I never criticized him, but in telling stories about my own childhood I cast Buck as an interesting character of sorts, which is, ironically, exactly how he would choose to portray himself.

"Hi there, young lady," he said.

"Hello," she said.

He brought Jean in. She seemed like a nice older woman; she was a primly dressed grandmotherly type. Buck said that he thought they'd stay in the village overnight and sleep in the van, parked in front of my sister's house. Jean looked to be in her seventies, and I wondered if she would go for sleeping overnight in my father's delivery van. By nightfall, they were gone. He and Jean didn't last long—I think her children intervened.

Pat was next.

I first heard about my father's latest wife in a phone call from my sister. News of our father traveled through the family in a circuitous, seemingly random fashion. After we had delivered bulletins about our gardens, kids, cousins, and the latest fight with the school board, a sentence or two about Buck would occasionally bubble to the surface, lumped in with the "in other news" section of the broadcast. Rachel didn't know much, only that Buck had gotten married. Again.

Dad popped in with Pat unannounced later that summer. Emily let them in and hovered in the background while I served coffee and he talked manically.

Buck said that he had started keeping bees and was selling honey. He told me that he and Pat lived in the farmhouse she grew up in and had inherited from her father. In the fall, during deer-hunting season, Pat ran a boardinghouse for the hunters who descended on the area to kill game on the state land just across from their house.

Then suddenly, as was his practice, he jumped up, said, "Well, it's time to go," took Pat by the arm, and left.

"What just happened?" Emily asked me.

My father just happened, is what.

I didn't see or hear from Buck again for several years, when he called to say that he had shot a bear and had to go to court. He said he wanted to tell me the story and I knew I wanted to hear it, but it took three months before I could get out to Port Allegheny.

I decided to make the trip on the day after Thanksgiving. Emily was with her dad in New York City for their annual Macy's Day Parade and dysfunctional family extravaganza. I thought it would be best if she were spared being exposed to my father on his own home territory; he had a tendency to live in what I thought were depressing and chaotic conditions, and I felt a twinge of embarrassment. After celebrating Thanksgiving at my cousin's house on Main Street, I left early the next morning for the drive to Port Allegheny. The cartoon topography of low hills and valleys around Freeville was awash in tints of brown and gray; it was Andrew Wyeth season, a sadly depressing time of year brightened, for some, only by the prospect of venicide. Gunfire rang out all morning in the fields surrounding the village and Toads diner was filled with camouflaged deer killers swapping hangover lies over their morning coffee.

I figured that if I made it out of my home county alive and raced for the state border, I had a chance of making the trip without being taken down by a stray bullet. As I neared Port Allegheny, I stopped for coffee at a gas station and saw in the local paper that no bears were killed in Port Allegheny during the short season; my father's off-season August kill had been the only bear killed by man in the area all year.

I crossed the Allegheny River at the edge of town, following my father's directions. The country was rough and rolling and it reminded me of him. I knew my father's place immediately from the number of vehicles in various states of repair parked beside and behind the house.

A large flatbed truck pulled up close behind my car on the road and followed me into the driveway. My father eased himself out of the cab and jumped to the ground. At seventy-two, he still had the Glenn Ford vestiges about him, but he had a noticeable limp and looked as if his life of hard labor had more or less caught up with him. "Ummmm, I gotta go do a job," he said as he waved my way. "It shouldn't take too long, so you can wait here." As usual, I wondered if he was struggling to remember my name. (He had a habit of never addressing any of his children by name, and we had all become accustomed to being called "Hey You" or "Hey Kid.")

I asked Buck what he had to do, and he said he had to move a building for some guys he knew. I asked if I could come along and he said, "Umm. Yeah. Sure." I climbed into the truck, and we rumbled back in the direction I had just come, back over the river and down the highway.

I hadn't ridden in the cab of a truck with my father for thirty years, but the sensation of jouncing along, high off the road beside my old man, surrounded by the detritus of his work life—the discarded receipts and gritty unpaid bills, along with the smell of tobacco and spilled coffee—was instantly familiar. I liked it. I admired his truck. He told me it was made in Brazil and that it was a goddamn workhorse. I asked him how big the building he had been hired to move was. He said he wasn't sure, but he didn't think it was too big. I asked him how much he was making for the job, and he said $50. "Jesus, Dad, that doesn't sound like very much money to move a building. Do you know how far you have to take it?" He said he didn't know but he didn't think it was too far. He had already gone to the Sears store forty miles away to pick up a water heater for someone that morning—this second job would help to pay for the truck.

Buck turned the flatbed down a narrow road and into a tidy trailer park. Three big guys were waiting for him, leaning against a decorative split-rail fence. Two of them sported mountain man beards and were taking pulls off quart-size bottles of iridescent green Mountain Dew. It was a cold day, and they looked like robo-men pounding down radiator fluid. The building in question was a large prefab garden shed with faux barn doors. The doors were decorated with crisscross timbers, such as you see in Mickey Rooney/Judy Garland movies. One look at it and I had an instant hankering to put on a show.

The owner of the shed had sold it to a woman a few miles down the road—all my father had to do was get it there. Buck produced seventy-five feet of heavy chain, and while the other men were encircling the shed with the chain, he expertly backed the flatbed close to the operation and then tipped the bed at an angle so the end was touching the ground. Then they hooked the chain to a winch and slowly hoisted the shed onto the bed of the truck. The other men pushed from the back, grunting directions as they exerted themselves.

I kept picturing little minidisasters of the kind I remember from my childhood, like the time my father sent us kids into the woods with one match apiece to build a campfire, and the one fire—his—was caught by a shifting wind and burned down an acre of brush. Or the time my father decided to speculate on sugar beets and planted forty acres of this particular "crop of the future" instead of our usual corn crop. That summer we had a drought and the sugar beets didn't come up, but the weeds did. Dad sent us kids into the field with a picture of a sugar beet plant to pull weeds and try to spot some seedlings, but there were none. Or the time he was going to outsmart the Arabs and bury a huge tank in our back pasture and fill it with oil. The tank sat in the pasture, large enough to become a local landmark and eyesore, rusting away in the weather until my mother had to pay someone to haul it away.

The shed operation was going smoothly, and I felt a bubble of pride as I climbed back into the cab of the truck. We were moving a building. It was here, and we were taking it down the highway to there. Fifty bucks for less than an hour's work seemed like a good deal, and as we rolled down the highway, I told my father so.

We met up with the other men who had helped load the shed onto the truck in another trailer park about ten miles down the highway. Sliding the shed off the truck and into position near one of the trailer homes was easy, with various residents of the neighborhood gathering around to watch the operation. One of the robo-men pulled out his wallet and gave my dad fifty dollars, and I climbed back into the cab of my father's truck to leave.

We were inches from a clean getaway in the big Brazilian flatbed when its back wheels started to spin, digging themselves into the soft ground up to their hubcaps. Pieces of plywood were produced and wedged beneath the wheels for traction. This method held great promise and actually looked as if it might work for the entire hour we spent arranging and rearranging the wood. I stood behind the flatbed, put my shoulder to its back rim, and we rocked and pushed the truck as my father jammed it into gear, only to have it slide back into the mud with each filthy pendulum swing.

The language of those surrounding the truck started to get salty. Men walked off in various directions to get more chain, and I acquainted myself with the woman who had bought the shed, who had come out to watch. As a full team member now, I felt some responsibility to distract her from the flatbed truck burying itself in her front yard, though she had the calm forbearance of someone who has seen worse and whose expectations were roughly equal to the scene. She cuddled her little dog—a licky bichon frise—

and told me about her son, who had spent most of his life in a wheelchair and then recently died.

A decision grew organically among the group that the flatbed truck would have to be towed, rather than pushed, out. A guy ran off and came back driving his brand-new two-ton pickup that frankly looked like a toy next to the old Brazilian workhorse. The owner of the truck proudly gunned his engine, and Buck silently took his place behind the wheel of the flatbed as a chain was hooked to its undercarriage and attached to the trailer hitch of the new pickup.

I noticed that my father was leaving the scheming to the other men and was standing more or less passively by as they engineered their wacky solutions. My father had been trapped in more than a few quagmires in his time. He had been towed and had done the towing. I wanted him to pipe up in the dominating know-it-all way I remembered. I wanted him to hearken back to the incident with the International and the snowbank, circa 1972. But it occurred to me that a lifetime of muddy mishaps and vehicular screwups might have tired him out. He looked like he wanted to call AAA. He looked like a guy who would gladly hand over his newly earned $50 in order to get out of this woman's yard and be home for lunch.

The brand-new pickup gunned and thrusted and blew blue smoke from its shiny chrome tailpipe. Its front wheels started to lift precariously off the ground like a show pony at a rodeo. At the same time its back wheels dug themselves into the mud up to their customized hubcaps. Now both vehicles were stuck. The Brazilian flatbed sat lumpen and bored in its ruts, mumbling to itself in Portuguese. Another group confab. Another guy ran out of the trailer park and across the road to a small farm. Barn doors opened. A cherry red antique tractor came speeding out of the barn and across the road. More deliberation. Should the pickup and the tractor be hitched side by side, each towing the Brazilian flatbed in a flanking maneuver (see fig. 1)? The merits of this were discussed and discarded. Instead, the tractor was hitched to the

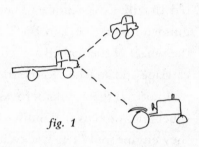

fig. 1

pickup, which was hitched to the flatbed, tug-of-war style (see fig. 2). The tractor would pull out the pickup, which would gain traction and pull out the flatbed. The scheme had a certain unlikely schoolyard beauty to it. It was the scene in the movie where the doubter smacks his head and says, "It's so crazy it might just work!"

fig. 2

Ideas like this are why country people are always on disability. Their access to chains and tractors combined with low education levels, innate strength, and a certain plucky courage make for a population who will drive fifty miles for an ice-cream cone and who think that a toy tractor can tow a two-ton pickup, which can in turn tow an obstinate

Brazilian flatbed truck piloted by a worn-out bear killer and his estranged daughter.

Gears grinding. More blue smoke. The red tractor reared up on its back wheels like an angry stallion, pulling at the pickup. Ten people mashed together shoulder to shoulder behind the Brazilian flatbed, pushing.

I pictured the trip to the hospital. Would they have an ambulance big enough for all of us, or would some of the more gravely injured have to hitch rides with the lesser injured? And if the nearest Sears was forty miles away, where was the hospital? I wondered if the bichon frise would licky-licky my face while I lay in the mud with a broken back. I wondered if being thrown clear of the wreckage was preferable to impalement, which would be quick and dramatic.

Somehow, in defiance of the family track record, flawed engineering principles, and the congenital and persistent bad luck of everyone involved, fortune smiled on us that chilly November day and delivered all three vehicles from the lawn of the bichon frise lady with the sad story and the new shed. Once we were free of the mud, the other participants in our adventure waved and disappeared into their trailer homes, and Buck and I started back to his house. We'd spent three hours moving the shed and the profit margin had sunk to familiar levels.

We had made enough money to pay for gas.

Pat was waiting for us in her yellow farmhouse. I walked past the woodstove and comfy chair, the gun rack and big TV, and into her large kitchen. She had three boarders at the house for hunting season—a band of hunter-brothers from Ohio. I heard gunfire ring out occasionally, bounce back and forth off the hills and carom through the valley. Pat would skin, dress, and cook any small game they brought back, and they would eat it for dinner that night. As Pat made her way from the stove to the table, she said in her no-nonsense way that whatever they killed, she'd find a way to cook it. She could make a squirrel stew or a pheasant pie, she said. I pictured a dinner of wolverine compote accompanied by muskrat wine and followed by bluebird cookies.

Over tuna sandwiches at the kitchen table, Buck started to tell the bear story. He produced some papers, which he said illustrated his claim of self-defense. The bear wasn't his fault, he said. The bear was the bear's fault. But I had a feeling that both creatures were simply being true to their nature.

Buck told me he first saw the bear when it ambled down off the ridge in back of the house and helped itself to a garbage can of cat food on the back porch. Here in his kitchen I noticed that he had at least two cats that periodically curled around his ankles as he talked. My father, the cat man.

Buck said that after the bear helped himself to the Friskies, he scrambled back up the ridge and disappeared into a stand of trees.

It was a male. Young. Big. My father said he was a beauty. He saw a tag pinned to the bear's ear—this wasn't the bear's first taste of kibble; it had been caught and tagged before by the game warden. Buck had a feeling that this bear had been released into their backwoods the previous week.

He called the game warden. The warden came out, and together they set and baited a barrel trap with rotted meat and honey. The warden told him to fortify his hives. My father spent the morning installing fencing at the apiary. As he told me this, he gestured out to the field in back of the house, where wooden trays of beehives stacked waist high were surrounded by a low electrified fence. It looked like a stalag in miniature. I pictured groups of worker bees smoking cigarettes and hanging around the prison yard, planning their escape from the queen.

As my father described his efforts to guard his bees from the bear, I found myself wondering why the bees didn't just fly out of their hives, group themselves into a giant flyswatter formation, and swat the bear away. Or they could just fly down his red bear trousers. Then I realized that all my knowledge about the interplay between bears and bees came from Hanna–Barbera cartoons.

After working on the fencing all morning, he and Pat had gone into town. On their way back to the house, a neighbor who kept goats flagged them down and said that the bear was back and had been lying in the road. The neighbor had to get out of his car and kick him to get him out of the road. "That bear wasn't afraid of anything. He was crazy," my father said.

Buck raced back to the hives to finish the fence. He said the bear was watching him from the edge of the tree line.

That's when my father's instincts, running as they do toward the harebrained, violent, and adventuresome, made him decide to take matters into his own hands, so he went and got his twenty-gauge shotgun.

When Buck got to this next part of the story, he started to sound wounded and practiced, like a man on the witness stand. He said he called the game warden a second time. Whatever. He got tired of the whole business.

The next time the bear came down the ridge, my father was waiting for him.

He says he waited until the bear got close enough—about twenty-five feet—and then he shot him in the chest.

The wounded bear fell down but then managed to scramble back into the woods.

That's when the game warden showed up. He asked my father what happened to the bear.

Buck said I just shot him.

They went into the woods and found the bear, crumpled in a heap—dead.

The officer wrote him up a ticket. Buck showed me the receipt. I recalled how my father had always railed against the system. He was a refusenik when it came to taxes, licenses, permits, paperwork, child support, insurance, credit cards, and savings accounts. Somehow he managed to square his feelings enough to cash his Social Security checks, but paying for a dead bear—that's where he drew his imaginary line.

Buck decided not to pay his $800 fine—two dollars per pound of bear.

He fought the fine in court. He called one lawyer who said she wouldn't take the case because she sided with the bear. He retained the services of an old, retired lawyer in town. I pictured the two of them shambling up the steps of a courthouse, each wearing his only suit, my father managing to look somehow handsome with his necktie knotted thickly against his throat.

The argument was self-defense. The young bear, a menace, not only destroying his hives but also charging down the hill at him. My father was being scrappy, his favorite attitude.

The judge said they could take payment for the fine in the form of a money order.

There would be an appeal. My father pulled out some papers to show me and started shuffling through them. There was a precedent. He thought a lawyer for the Farm Bureau over in Harrisburg might agree to represent him.

I asked my father if he'd learned anything from killing the bear. I asked him if he saw the bear as a metaphor for something else and if he could explain that to me. The questions I really wanted answers for went unasked. I wanted to know who he was, what he longed for, and why he left all those years ago—cleaving my childhood in two.

"Ummmm, Jesus. I don't see things as metaphors for other things," he said.

I asked Pat what she thought of all of this. She said she had cooked bear meat before and that it could be very tasty as long as it was young and not old and tough.

My father walked me to the car. We had spent the bulk of the day together. I realized that in my whole life, I had never spent so many hours all at once with him.

We said good-bye, and Pat came out. I waved to them both as I drove away.

I wondered if I would ever see the old man again. I guessed there was a chance I wouldn't.

I reflexively looked in the rearview mirror, but he was already gone.

I called Emily from the car. "Well, did Buck really kill a bear?" she asked. I told her the story. She sighed and laughed. She only knew her grandfather over the years through my telling, but she said to me, "Mommy, this sounds just like him, doesn't it?"

"I guess it does. And now I'm wishing that you had been here with me, because I want you to know about some of the stuff you're made of. I want you to see how some people really live—and it's not pretty. Sometimes, it's just one disaster after another."

Fortunately, Emily and I were lucky enough to be surrounded by family members who were disaster specialists. In our world, it was the women who grabbed shovels and push brooms and swept up after the tempests that periodically blew down our house.

My father doesn't see things as metaphors for other things, but I do. As I drove back home to Freeville, I tried not to think about the jobs, the wives, the children he left and the grandchildren he would never know, but about the bees and the honey they make. The honey stands for the sweetness of life, while the bee brings the sting. My father, the self-aggrandizing bear killer, was both the bee and the honey to me.

ELEVEN

This Too Shall Pass

M Y FIRST EXTENDED fantasy about taking Emily to college happened when she was three years old. She was flipping out in the parking lot of an Applebee's restaurant somewhere in Maine at the time. We were on a long road trip from Freeville to Auburn, Maine, and by hour eight, she had had it. She wheeled and careened, running away from me through the parking lot, screaming and throwing herself onto the pavement. The serpentine slow-speed chase ended in a row of bushes just next to the windows lining the restaurant. I caught her and tried to hold on as she squirmed and arched her back, like a cat on its way to the vet. Diners watched us through the windows with alternating looks of compassion and disgust as I wrestled my daughter into the mulch.

Mom, who was taking this trip with us, went ahead into the restaurant. When I was finally able to carry Emily in, my mother looked at her granddaughter's blotchy face and tear-struck eyes and said, "How is she?"

"It's more like, *who* is she, and the answer is, Linda Blair."

I wondered if there was a military academy somewhere in the Maine woods that would accept an oversize toddler with anger management issues. I had it all figured out. I would drop Emily off along with her *Beauty and the Beast* backpack. Then I would drive quickly away and go to a roadside diner, sit at the counter, and eat a big piece of pie. All by myself.

"It's a stage," my mother said. My mother always said that. From her seasoned perspective, everything was a stage. I often thought my mother should write a parenting book summing up her childrearing methods called *It's a Stage*. It wouldn't be much of a book, frankly, because her philosophy pretty much consisted of "This too shall pass." Really, it would be more of a one-page handout, like the smeary Xerox of the cabbage soup diet that kept circulating among my friends. My mother's parenting book would have to wait until she wrote her cookbook, however. She had long planned to share her secrets to country cooking but for now had only the title: *After the Cat Has Licked It*.

Like any parent who was learning on the job, I lacked two things: experience and perspective. I could imagine

Emily physically growing (she was already an accomplished grower), but I couldn't imagine her changing. I could only picture her as an eighteen-year-old toddler—six feet tall, out of control, careening her way through a tantrum, and wearing Depends.

Fortunately for both of us, Emily both grew *and* changed, and when the time came to say good-bye I had mastered the basics of motherhood and was deeply in love with her— after all, my inability to find an appropriately grown-up romantic partner meant that the kid and I had essentially been dating for eighteen years. It follows then that I would try to subvert her dreams by urging her to stay home, or at least in the vicinity of home, through her college years. Her response was to be interested only in schools at least five hundred miles away from Chicago or Freeville.

Emily navigated the lengthy passage of college prep with her customary calm. Her high school started revving up in the sophomore year, terrifying most of the kids and throwing gasoline onto the burning embers of their anxious parents' college ambitions. For me, almost every contact with other parents, no matter how glancing, became an unbearable conversation about the ABCs of college, which to me seemed little more than an opportunity to brag about the prospects of our offspring. As the mother of an academically average student who didn't speak Chinese or play the violin and who had never, not once, built housing for the poor in Costa Rica, I didn't really want to go there. Mainly I avoided the topic and tried to dodge queries because nothing I had to say mattered, and I was susceptible to sustained— though mainly private—freak-outs.

It started when I encountered a mom I knew in the school parking lot in the middle of a school day. She mentioned that she was taking Amber out of school that afternoon to go see a private tutor for PPSAT test prep.

I didn't know what the PPSAT was, but I knew what the SAT was, and I took this whole tutoring business as a sign that Emily was already behind. I have spent the majority of my motherhood playing catch-up to the moms who have their acts together, so this sinking feeling was a familiar fist to the gut. This would be a replay of the famous "you're too late to sign up for ballet" incident of 1995.

When I saw Emily after school that day, I peppered her: Was she preparing for the PPSAT, and if not, why not? Did she need a tutor, and if so, would she go to one? If she didn't go to a PPSAT tutor, would she end up slinging garlic knots at a Pizza Hut, not that there's anything wrong with that?

Emily spoke slowly, the way you might to a mental patient. "The PPSAT is a practice test for the PSAT."

"And? So?" I offered, helpfully.

"The PSAT is the practice test for the SAT," she said.

My mind was a blank.

"So you want me to get a tutor to practice for the practice test of the practice test?" she asked.

Well, actually—no. Even I know how dumb *that* is.

My anxiety had a focus: I was worried that Emily wouldn't get into college. I was also worried that she would.

I knew she must leave me. I wondered if I could possibly stop her.

Emily showed up on time for the precollege tests she needed to take. She sought out her college counselor for solo sessions. We visited several campuses together—our tours became a blur of backward-walking student guides talking about the wonders of the meal plan and their awesome classes, attractive and accessible professors, and totally fun roommates. Our most memorable visit was a trip we took to Williamsburg, Virginia, to see the College of William and Mary. Emily and I had been to Colonial Williamsburg before—on a tourist trip when she was nine years old. On that trip we indulged our geeky love of old-timey costumes and strolled up and down the Duke of Gloucester Street wearing bonnets and eating salty/sweet kettle corn, a treat I would place at the tippy top of my personal food pyramid. Nine years later, the college visit happened on an exquisite day; Emily went on a campus tour while I lay on the grass of the college's great lawn, pondering her departure and the mysteries of my life beyond.

Emily raced home to the mailbox during her lunch period every day for two weeks in March of her senior year. She received her share of fat and skinny envelopes and in the end chose to go to William and Mary. The kettle corn in Colonial Williamsburg might have been the deciding factor, though the prospect of bonnet wearing while taking a work-study job as a butter churner was a definite inducement.

Our good-bye was long, sustained—and involved lots of

plastic bins. I can't think of what we all did before we had the ability to hermetically seal our belongings in plastic, but I seem to remember it involved old suitcases and those big black trunks with the flimsy locks that also doubled as dorm room coffee tables. Now it was all Tupperware.

Emily and I packed her room in Chicago along with other assorted furniture and our gigantic green balloon-tire bikes, shoved Chester the cat into his carrier, and drove east to Freeville for our summer of good-byes. I thought of my father as I climbed up into the large beat-up moving van I had rented for the trip and navigated it through downtown Chicago. My old man's legacy to me was not only my congenital jackassiness, but also the natural-born ability to drive a truck.

In Freeville we mark the passage of summer by watching the corn grow. When Emily and I left for a long-promised week in Paris in late June, the corn was shin high in the fields surrounding the village. In Paris, Emily tried out her high school French while I talked. Loudly. And. Slowly. In. English. Eventually I learned to ask simple questions in French while not understanding one word of the answers. Emily was able to get her hands on an English version of the newest and last Harry Potter book and read it obsessively while we lingered, dreamily, at cafés. Then in the afternoons she read aloud to me while I rested and attempted to recover from my jet lag (I never did). The first Harry Potter book came out when Emily was eight, and I had read the adventure aloud to her. Now her childhood was bookended by her favorite characters, who seemed to grow and change at exactly the same rate she did. Now she was reading to me.

In Freeville, we rode bikes, kayaked on the creek, and went "porch visiting"—setting out from our house on Main Street and spending the day roaming from porch to porch—from grandmother to cousins to sisters to aunts—admiring gardens and drinking iced tea. Every other Saturday morning, the men's barbecue committee at the Methodist Church fired up their long trough of coals in the barbecue pit across from the church and set the marinated birds breast to wing on the long grill. When the meat started to cook, its vinegary scent drifted through the village, and we knew what we'd be eating for dinner.

The corn grew into great tall stalks and the fields looked densely packed, rippling and lush. It ripened early, and so starting the first week of August, we ate it every night—and then, abandoning any pretext of nutritional balance, went to an all-corn diet while it lasted. We compared varieties—was the Baby Sweet really as sweet as the Butter N Sugar? We were partial to the bicolored varieties with small, pale kernels. It tasted more like candy than a vegetable. I'd cook up a dozen ears at night and put the leftovers on a plate in the refrigerator, snack on it late at night, and eat a cold cob for breakfast along with my coffee.

One or two nights a week if the weather was fine, I pulled out our projector and Emily would set it up in the backyard. We arranged two rows of chairs in the grass—

Adirondack chairs, twig chairs, dining room chairs, and two easy chairs from the living room—invited the family over, and played our favorite movies projected against the back of our white house. I let Emily program our summertime film festival, and she chose *The Philadelphia Story*, *Desk Set*, *Some Like It Hot*, and other black-and-white favorites. The tinny vintage soundtracks drifted over our little backyard and mingled with the sounds of traffic on Main Street. Mornings after a movie night while starting out for my early workday, I would look out the kitchen window to see cast-off lap blankets and gnawed-over corncobs lying in the dew. Popcorn littered the grass like snowflakes.

Wednesday mornings—*every* Wednesday morning—we met our family at the Queen Diner in Dryden. After Toads diner closed the summer before, we experienced exactly six days of mourning and then switched our weekly family breakfast meetings to the Queen, three miles away. Aunts Lena, Millie, and Jean, cousins Nancy and Lorraine, Rachel, Emily, Mom, and I crowded around a too-small table and took up our long-running family conversation—which was always already in progress.

At the Queen, we each ordered our regular breakfasts, and Judy, our waitress, patiently wrote out separate checks for our meals and left the checks in a pile on the table. My family is incapable of performing the subtraction required to split a check; they are also unwilling to let one person pick up the check, so every Wednesday Judy writes out ten checks in amounts ranging from $1.56 to $3.48, including tax. My mother and aunts always leave their tips in embarrassing little piles of coins beside each plate, and I follow suit when I'm with them because I don't want to be too show-offy.

Emily and I were excited about driving down to Virginia to drop her off at college. She was going over her list of college supplies at the table. We had brought a road atlas with us to review the route with Mom and the aunties. As usual, the conversation circled and wheeled around and never touched down for long.

My aunt Lena turned to me. "So, what day will you be back from your trip?" she asked. I could tell this wasn't an idle question. First of all, Aunt Lena had never been one to ask an idle question. Compared to the opinionated bigmouths of the rest of the women of the family, Aunt Lena, the eldest of the group, had a tendency to listen and chuckle. I had an extraordinary affection for her, not only because of her skills as an audience member, but also because her natural reserve often made me wonder what she was thinking.

Because of a perfect storm of scheduling conflicts among the middle generation of my family, I knew that for the next couple of weeks I would be the only family member in Freeville over the age of twelve and under seventy-five with a valid driver's license. At the Queen, over the jumble of coffee cups and egg-smeared plates, Aunt Lena looked at me expectantly. I had the distinct impression that she saw a giant steering wheel where my head should be. She didn't even really have to ask. I knew that the day after dropping

Emily off at college, I would be driving Aunt Lena and her husband of sixty-nine-and-three-quarters years, my uncle Harvey, to the VA Hospital in Syracuse. After a long life-time of good health, Harvey had developed heart problems, followed by surgery, followed by that ominous medical catchall known as "complications."

My mother and her oldest sister were slowing down. The circumference of their world had shrunk to a roughly fifteen-mile circuit along familiar roads. Syracuse, an hour away along an interstate, was too much and too far to travel. Where I had once scheduled my time according to work commitments and travels with Emily, now I started keeping track of who among the older generation of my family needed to go somewhere. I told Lena I'd make sure to be back from Virginia in time to make the next appointment.

Emily chose to say good-bye by riding her bike slowly around the village, waving languidly at the school, post of-fice, and swing sets on the playground. Then before driving out of town in the morning, we pulled into Mom's drive-way, and she came out and stood on her porch, leaning on her cane. "So long, my dear," she said. (My mother never says "good-bye." She only says "so long.")

"So long, Mom, I'll write to you," Emily said, and I knew she would.

I had reserved the long drive to Virginia for the convey-ance of a thoughtful lecture series I intended to deliver to my daughter with talks on topics such as "Your Body and You," "The Hidden Menace of Credit Card Debt," "Roommates:

The Good, the Bad and the Bipolar," and "The Temptation of On-Campus ROTC Recruiters." Emily, sensing what she was in for, deflected me with Top 40 tunes and frequent Dunkin' Donuts stops. Two hours from campus, feeling that our time was running out, I said to her, "There's so much I want to tell you. I feel like I need to tell you important things about life."

"Mommy, I'm not—I'm not going out to sea. I'm just going to college. I'll call you with important questions about life and then you can answer them, how's that?"

The southern scenery blurred by. I could see the massive trees thickly lining the interstate drooping and wilting in the heat.

"Hey," Emily offered. "Can you list your five favorite books?"

"Ooooh. Good question. Well played, honey."

Emily knew that the whole Edith Wharton/Virginia Woolf relative-ranking issue would soak up much of our remaining time together.

The August day was airless and southern-sweaty hot. Our hair stuck itself flat against our foreheads in moist clumps. I took Emily to her brick dorm and parked the car while she introduced herself to her two roommates. One, from China, didn't have any parents with her to distract her; she sat quietly on her bed and told us she had video Web-chatted with her mother in Beijing that morning. The other roommate had two parents in the small room, and they were expressing their anxiety by talking very loudly and quickly about buying more fans (there was no air-conditioning) and rearranging the furniture. Emily and I unloaded her things, and I left her in the room and went to walk around campus, where I saw hundreds of families doing the exact same dance—unloading vans of Tupperware and trying to keep their feelings as tightly sealed as their possessions.

When I got back to her dorm, Emily's father had arrived from New York and was trying to stand out of the way in the small and crowded room. We said a fond hello, as we always did, and I was reminded of how we had met, almost thirty years before—in a similar setting on a campus during my own first days of college. He offered to run out to a hardware store to get duct tape or shelving or a throw pillow, and Emily let him.

Later that afternoon the three of us escaped the stifling room and walked to a bookstore in the village. He and I sat and had iced coffee while Emily shopped for some last-minute school supplies. My ex and I first met over books, we fell in love over (and on top of) books, and I was enchanted when we were students that he kept a very neat list in a ledger of every book he had ever read. We still found it easy to talk about work and what we were watching on television and what we were reading and writing. He congratulated me on my professional success, and I thanked him. I asked about his wife and kids, and he told me. We traded stories about our parents' illnesses and said we were mutually sorry that they were suffering.

Over the years, my ex-husband and I had maintained our easy rapport. Here's how we did our divorce: *nicely.* While he was talking I wondered if this was one of the last encounters the two of us would ever have. I could imagine seeing him at a graduation ceremony, perhaps a funeral, and maybe, someday, a wedding, but the string connecting us had slackened, and I hadn't felt its tug in a very long time. In the early days of our breakup, I used to force myself not to call him. Like an addict subscribing to a 12-step program, at the end of each long day I would lie in bed and congratulate myself for not dialing his number that day and promise myself not to dial his number the next day. Now I considered erasing him from my cell phone's address book because with our child away from home and without the need to coordinate visits, I couldn't imagine why I would ever call him. Emily had entered his four phone numbers in my phone under the heading DAD.

"Well, this is it," he said.

"Yes, I guess it is," I said.

"She's great," he said, gesturing toward Emily.

"I'm excited for her," I said.

"You've done a good job, Amy," he offered.

"Well, she was easy to raise," I said.

Me? Not so much. Raising me hasn't exactly been a picnic.

Emily's college had thoughtfully planned separate activities for the parents and the students—no doubt this was to start the process of prying apart the embrace. Emily went off to bond with her roommates, my ex-husband went to his hotel, and I participated in a humiliating scavenger hunt that may or may not have also been a cocktail party. I was reminded of how activities and drinking are combined at college in ways you don't see out in the world.

The next morning I met Emily for breakfast in the school's cafeteria, and she told me she really liked her room-mates and couldn't wait to get started. She had a full day of orientation activities ahead of her. I was going to shove off.

We walked quietly arm in arm to my car. She looked down at me from her full height and said, "Mommy, you're going to be fine."

I looked up at her. My little girl was now a head taller than I. "I know I'll be fine, my dear, and you are going to be fine too."

I decided that until that fine day when we would both be fine, I would firmly seal my feelings in Tupperware.

Emily opened the car door and placed me in the front seat in the manner you see the cops doing to perps on TV—with a protective hand atop my head so I wouldn't graze it on the doorframe.

And then she reached in through the car's open window, hugged me around the neck, and said, "It's called Match .com, Mom. You just type in your zip code and a list of guys pops up."

"Right, right, I love you too, kid," I said, and drove away. She waved to me until she was a dot in the rearview mirror, and I stared at her until she disappeared like an apparition into the shimmering landscape of her new home.

I took back roads up through Virginia and back to DC. That night I stayed at Gay's house in Washington, and she looked at me tenderly and poured me a glass of wine. Gay had recently taken up African drumming, and even though I would rather stick needles in my eyes than learn a new instrument, when she pulled her two djembe drums out from the corner and taught me some simple rhythms, I felt I was communicating with my dear friend in a new, wonderful, and wordless way. Gay was Emily's first teacher in nursery school and had watched her grow. Her two children, now both in college, were as dear to me as any of my many nieces and nephews. Gay and I had a pact that we would live together as spinster ladies when we got old—though we both openly hoped it wouldn't come to that.

I waited for a wave of something—anything—to prove how much I was missing and mourning Emily, but it wouldn't come. While I wasn't looking, my girl reached out and grabbed her adulthood. We had shared her childhood, and her job now was to leave home, and my job was to let her. I couldn't imagine returning to my empty house except to assume that I would drown my loneliness in merlot, family, and television sitcoms. As I drove due north toward Freeville I concentrated on holding the tears at bay while I tried to redirect my attention to the other women in my life.

Because now it was their turn.

TWELVE

I'll Fly Away

MY UNCLE HARVEY has the sleep schedule of a honeybee. He goes to bed at seven o'clock and gets up at 2 A.M., fully rested and ready to pollinate after seven hours of deep sleep. Harvey's most potent and wide-awake hours are in the deepest shank of the night. While the rest of the world enjoys the fruits of the REM cycle—romping in their dream life with puppies or Pierce Brosnan—Uncle Harvey will drink a pot of coffee, read his Bible, and watch Fox News until sunup. He starts fading at around noon, so he wisely always tries to grab the first medical appointment of the day.

The morning after I returned from taking Emily to college in Virginia, I went downstairs at 6 A.M. to discover Aunt Lena and Uncle Harvey waiting patiently in the driveway for me to drive them to the VA hospital in Syracuse. I wondered if they had slept in their car.

As we drove toward Syracuse, I chitchatted with my aunt and uncle about the lovely rolling farmland bordering the Mohawk Valley. I told them about my trip to drop off Emily at college and said she had already called and was settling in. We watched the sun rise together.

At the hospital, Harvey went in for his appointment and Lena and I settled into our chairs in the waiting room. I set up my laptop and tried to work; Lena leafed through a magazine and eventually fell asleep, holding her purse on her lap.

Aunt Lena seemed tired. Lately, all the older women in my life seemed sort of tired. I worried about them. They worked and raised families. They deserved to put their feet up—my mother, especially, because she did it alone.

Unfortunately, the rheumatoid arthritis she suffered from for the last twenty years has disabled her in heartbreaking degrees. Now my sisters and I struggle to find ways to make her life easier. I do her shopping and some nights cook dinner for her, and we watch CNN together. We visit, talk about books, go to the movies, and take drives through the countryside. I try to do for her some of the same things she's done for me, and I didn't even realize I had become good at it until we were at dinner recently and I leaned over and cut her meat for her, the way you do when your kids are little and you don't even think about it.

I knew my priorities had really changed the day I skipped a conference call with my lawyer to take my mother's cat to the vet to be shaved. You might wonder why a cat needs to be shaved, or who could possibly make enough money to shave cats for a living. I too had all of these questions. (The answers are: (1) mats and burrs, and (2) no one makes enough money to shave cats for a living, but they do it anyway.)

My uncle Harvey needed to be taken to Syracuse a few more times over the course of the late autumn. His health seemed to improve a little between each trip, and I got so I looked forward to these outings. After the appointments, we made a point of stopping somewhere for a meal. My relatives usually travel in clumps, so seeing my aunt and uncle by themselves was a rare treat. Fortunately, over a creamy white lunch of chicken and biscuits followed by rice pudding, I thought to tell them both how much I was enjoying our time together.

In October, I went to Chicago on a business trip. Being out of Freeville for the first time in three months made me think. I'm pushing fifty. I've seen the world, but I'm living on the same tiny patch of land where I was born. I'm surrounded by people who are not impressed with me. They don't care that my syndicated column has twenty-two million readers, that I've been on the *Today* show—that I've locked horns with Bill O'Reilly, or that my name was once used as a clue on *Jeopardy!* They remember what a doofus I was in high school. My nemesis of thirty years ago from the cheerleading squad, "Pepper," works at the local ob/gyn office. When I saw her at our reunion last summer, she said, "Oh, Amy, you cut your hair."

I was a mediocre cheerleader. My heart was in it and I could yell plenty loudly, but my muscles, tendons, and cartilage were basically uncooperative. Seeing Pepper at the reunion, all I could think about was how I couldn't quite do a Russian split and how mean she was to me, three decades ago. "Yeah, Pepper, that's right," I replied frostily. "I did cut my hair. In 1982." (Given my luck, when it's time for me to get my next pap smear I have a feeling I know who will be snapping her gloves into place.)

I started thinking about my choices. What I mean is that I started to wonder if driving elderly people around or taking cats to be shaved was really a good use of my time. I still had a daily column to write and professional prospects to explore. I was still thinking about this on the way back from Chicago. I was driving back from the airport, headed back into my little hometown and back into our small lives. Despite my daughter's advice, I hadn't had a date in many moons. The last good kiss I had was years ago. Following Emily's directive after dropping her off at college I went on Match.com and typed in Freeville's zip code and the guys in the database looked—every last one of them—too familiar to me. I couldn't think of the last time I'd come home tipsy and decided to sleep in. On a recent Friday night, I found myself feeling kind of excited because my niece had a soccer game and I was going to go. For the first time in many weeks, I wore lipstick.

I returned from Chicago on a Tuesday night. The next morning, I called my mother to see if she wanted a ride to the Queen Diner, because it was Wednesday and that's what we do on Wednesdays. Rachel answered the phone. "Come down here," she said.

I raced to my mother's house. My aunt Millie, Rachel, and Mom were sitting in the living room. Aunt Millie asked me to sit down. Then she got tears in her eyes, and so Rachel took over. Rachel said that Aunt Lena had died of a heart attack the night before. Aunt Lena—she wasn't even sick. But then I thought about how tired she had looked, there in the hospital waiting room, sleeping with her purse in her lap.

Lena was eighty-five, and the death of an eighty-five-year-old woman can hardly be described as a tragedy. But it was a shock, and we started missing her immediately. Our family has been so blessed, it's almost embarrassing. The last family member to die passed away in 1966. That's over forty years of everybody waking up each morning, healthy.

Family members from all over the country converged in Freeville to celebrate and mourn. It was obvious that Lena had lived well because she was so loved. My aunt—she worked at the Freeville school cafeteria. She was a lunch lady. She also raised a family and then she raised a few of her grandchildren and she had rescued a few of her great-grandchildren. They were all there to thank her. She was something.

At the funeral at the Freeville United Methodist Church, my cousin Roger led the service, and Rachel, my cousin Jan, my niece Clara, and I performed as an auxiliary gene pool choir and sang the old gospel song "I'll Fly Away." During our rehearsal at the church I couldn't get through the song because my tears kept chasing the tune away. I asked Rachel how to sing it without crying. She gave me a tip: "You have to look down at the music. Don't look out at the congregation. If you look at them and see how sad they are, you're toast." But when the time came and we were gathered in front of the altar, standing in a little cluster overlooking my beloved aunt's casket, I realized that I couldn't *not* look at my family.

I found my mother sitting next to Anne in her usual pew. My mother, who never says "good-bye" but only says "so long," was still and expressionless. Her face was a stoic mask, but her gray eyes were red-rimmed and watery. That morning Mom had said to me, "I only wish I had known Lena better." I wondered how you could possibly know a person better whom you had been acquainted with for seventy-eight years and had seen almost daily for much of that time, but I think I understood what she meant. Lena was by far the most reserved of my aunts. And when you love people you always want to know them better.

We sang.

Some bright morning when this life is over
I'll fly away
To that home on God's celestial shore
I'll fly away
I'll fly away oh glory
I'll fly away (in the morning)
When I die hallelujah by and by
I'll fly away.

Aunt Millie stood up. She said she couldn't eulogize her sister. But then she said, simply, "We used to be four sisters, and now we are three."

I know it's a substantial and unique burden my generation faces. We can have babies until we're fifty years old and still our parents linger at the party—too healthy to give up this world. Studies show—and many letters to my column reflect—that this lifestyle of being sandwiched between needy generations is extremely hard on us. We miss work, we miss school, we miss having friendships and relationships because of our caregiving duties. We get sick, we get tired, and we wonder when we'll catch a break.

Here I am in advanced middle age and I finally realize what it means to be an adult. To give, with no possibility that I'll be rewarded. I used to think that being a parent defined my adulthood. *Mothering* was the making of me. But emotionally, mothering is little league caretaking; it's nothing compared to trying to keep these wonderful women in my life—knowing all the while that one day they will leave it.

Autumn took on its own beauty. I saw the leaves change and listened to the daily progress of hundreds upon hundreds of geese honking overhead as they headed south for the winter. I hadn't experienced fall in Freeville since graduating from high school. Football and soccer season heated up. I sat with Rachel in the shadow of our old alma mater and cheered for my niece, fourteen-year-old Clara. I painted the porch steps, put away the kayaks, and put my garden and my mother's garden to bed.

From my house on Main Street I watched the leaves dangle from the trees and drift to the ground in a rain of color. I spent the morning of my forty-eighth birthday raking them into giant mounds. I handed out candy from my front porch to a couple hundred ghosts, goblins, and little Paris Hiltons on Halloween, called Emily, and described the scene to her. I felt my usual seasonal craving for sharp cheese and maple syrup. On my occasional business trips to Chicago I wandered around our quiet apartment with its beautiful lake and city views and realized that I no longer really lived there. I had moved back home.

Emily and I sent letters back and forth—written on paper and sealed in envelopes. She described reading Boswell's *Life of Johnson*, and said, "Samuel Johnson reminds me of Bill Clinton." She was happy, and I was happy for her. I wrote back, describing how Chester the cat kept escaping off the porch and how one of these days I wasn't going to go after him and he could just see how he liked living on the street, reduced to dancing on the corner of Union and Main for

Friskies. I caught her up on the doings of her grandmother, aunts, and cousins. I described our most recent Wednesday breakfast at the Queen Diner and told her how her great-aunt's death had left an empty chair at our gatherings that I couldn't quite adjust to. I also told her I was seriously think-ing about renovating and enlarging our house in order to make it better suited for a permanent home.

My little house on Main Street was starting to feel too small. I wanted ten more feet upstairs, with a sleeping porch overlooking the creek. I could see it in my mind's eye. Some-times I pressed my hands against the wall of the back bed-room upstairs. *M-o-o-o-v-e*.

I called a local builder I knew and asked him to take a look at the house. I first met Bruno when I was in seventh grade. Over the years he had built up a successful business, and Emily and I would see signs bearing his name in front of construction projects and handsome historic houses around the county. We ran into him now and then with his daugh-ters at day camp, ice-skating, or over at Clark's Sure Fine Food Mart in Dryden. When I checked his company's Web site I noticed his motto: "Dreams built on time."

Bruno said he was happy to hear from me and that he'd meet me at the house to talk about the renovation project. He parked his truck in my driveway and came inside. He walked around my little place, went upstairs and down, grabbed a piece of paper and distractedly drew the floor plan.

"Well, what do you think?" I asked him. My voice was suddenly high-pitched and eager, like a chipmunk.

He looked me in the eye. *My, but his eyes are blue*, I thought. "Well, Amy. It's like this. This is a tiny house on a little lot right on the street. The renovation would cost more than the house is worth." He paused. "Now—some little houses are so special that it doesn't matter. You'll do whatever it takes to make them right."

I thought about the day Emily and I moved in and how the screen door came off in my hand as my family stood on the porch and watched. Every year I had done one thing that I could afford to improve the place, and by now it was on the verge of adorable. I was proud of my little house and happy that Bruno thought it was so special. He had a reputation for having impeccable taste.

He continued, ". . . This, however, is *not* one of those special houses. I think if you want a bigger house, you should probably move."

He asked if he could sit down, and I offered him coffee. He asked if I had heard about his divorce. I had not. He started to talk. He stayed a little longer, and then he stayed even longer after that.

After he left, I thought about him. Like everybody else in my hometown world, I've known him for most of my life. He was one of thirteen children who grew up on a dairy farm three miles from ours. After our own farm fell apart, my sisters and I spent part of every day during three successive summers at their house. Mom had gone to work full-time and our place was lonely and quiet, so we joined the herd of kids and livestock at their farm. We swam in the pond and ate chaotic suppers at their table. I remembered watching Bruno herd their Holsteins through the pasture and toward the barn for the evening milking. The harvest before my freshman year of high school, my sisters and I helped him and some of his many brothers and sisters stack hay bales in their barn.

Watching as Bruno drove away, I remembered exactly the way he looked in his high school basketball uniform in 1974—he was a rangy farm boy wearing a ponytail and short satin trunks. His legs were like springs, and he had a nice jump shot, but his strength was under the boards. Bruno was a scrappy rebounder and turnover specialist. I remembered him as being fast, strong, unpredictable, and hard to contain. Life seemed to have sanded down his edges, however. Now he seemed both strong and soft at the same time. I had a hankering to go after Bruno, to ask him to take a walk with me. I wanted us to play checkers and to sit at the kitchen table, reading the newspaper together. I wanted to go on a bike ride with him.

Snow was in the air, and I could smell the long northern winter on the horizon. Soon a new season would drift down and cover Main Street—and the fields, woods, and streams beyond—in a six-month blanket of white. In a couple of weeks, Emily would be coming home for Christmas. The day before I had pulled two pairs of ice skates from the closet—one for Emily and one for me—and placed them next to the front door.

It's funny how things happen. It was nothing like what

my friends had all told me over the years when they would try to worry me into a relationship: "Get out there! You'll never meet a guy in your living room!" they'd say. I took their advice and also reflected this take-charge philosophy in my advice column, telling singles to sign up for online dating sites and to take cooking classes. I have been single for seventeen years. I have stopped trying, I have started trying, and then I have given up all over again. I have forgotten and revived my adolescent crush on Donny Osmond in—golly—four decades.

And now, what do you know? It turns out you *can* meet a guy in your living room.

Wednesday morning came around. I was standing in the parking lot of the Queen Diner, about to join my family and resume our lifelong conversation. I pondered my options. I knew exactly what my mother, sister, cousins, aunts, and I would talk about. I pictured our little pile of separate checks and the tip coins next to the plates. I wondered if the women of my family would miss me at breakfast—just this once. I stared at my phone, nervously rehearsed my side of the conversation, and dialed Bruno's number. He answered on the first ring.

"I figured that since you turned down my renovation project, the least you could do is buy me a cup of coffee," I said to him.

"Where and when?" he asked.

I ran into the Queen and joined my family at the table. I

ordered coffee but no breakfast. Rachel asked why I was so antsy.

"I think I need to skip breakfast today," I said.

"What, you have to work?" my mother asked, rhetorically. (I had never missed Wednesday breakfast for work—or any other reason.)

Aunt Jean said, "Hot date?" Everyone except for me laughed.

"Um. I have to meet someone in Ithaca," I said.

"Well, I can't believe you're blowing off breakfast just to meet someone in Ithaca," Rachel said.

Then she looked at me. She knew. "But if you have to go, you have to go . . ."

As I reached behind me for my scarf and coat, Mom said, "Well, it's not like we won't see you later." One thing my family and I are really good at is seeing one another later. We've been seeing one another later for generations. And so on this day, I decided to cut short my weekly date with the women in my life, and with their grudging permission, I took a chance on having a Wednesday morning conversation with someone who doesn't share my DNA.

Bruno and I met and talked for a long time. We drank three gallons of coffee apiece. Then we drove out through town and into the countryside, past the hills, fields, and forests and through the landscape of our shared childhoods. He talked about raising his daughters alone, and I talked about raising my daughter alone. Between us we had five daughters, all in the throes of various stages of adolescence—his oldest and Emily were born exactly a week apart. Bruno told me the sad story of the ending of his marriage and I told him mine. We had both taken many years to figure out what had gone wrong.

He said, "I have an idea, Amy. Let's do everything differently this time."

WHEN EMILY CAME home for Christmas vacation, she walked into the house and said, "Wow, what's with all the flowers, Mommy?!" I replied with a sentence that, in all our life together, I had never once uttered to my daughter.

"Honey—I think I have a boyfriend!"

"I think I have a boyfriend too!" she said. He was a boy at college who had taken her out for coffee, movies, and dinner. "So, who's your boyfriend, anyway?" she asked. When I told her she said, "Bruno? Hubba hubba."

Over the next few weeks Bruno and I surrounded ourselves with our combined five daughters, sledding, skiing, skating, playing games, watching movies, and cooking together. I gingerly brought him around Mom and the aunties and they offered their hearty approval; at our next breakfast at the Queen, we clinked our coffee cups together and toasted this surprising romantic development.

Then, one frosty night, as we were standing together on the sidewalk, Bruno said that he was sorry he had declined to renovate my house—but then happily, he asked if he could renovate my life instead.

And I decided to let him.

1989, LONDON

2008, CHICAGO

For more information about Amy's Mighty Queens
and to share stories of the Mighty Queens in your life,
log on to www.mightyqueens.com.